100 … M

DISTRICT 1: CITY CENTRE

Most tourists don't make it further than the Kalverstraat, but the centre has so much more to offer. Surprise yourself with the cultural side of the Red Light District, rummage around in the countless (vintage) boutiques and discover the lesser-known side of Amsterdam.

DISTRICT 2: JORDAAN

The Jordaan remains the most fun, bustling and lively quarter. You can still hear the typical Amsterdam humour in the Noordermarkt and in the centuries-old cafés. Visit all the little 'hofjes' (almshouses with courtyard gardens), Anne Frank's house, the Westerkerk and the Haarlemmerstraat. Meet the real Amsterdam folk.

DISTRICT 3: NEGEN STRAATJES

Do you like shopping? The Negen Straatjes are packed with (clothing) boutiques and fantastic lunchrooms and restaurants for those much-needed snacks. If you want something new for your home – from kitsch to designer – visit the Rozengracht. The shops round the Spui are a bookworm's paradise.

DISTRICT 4: OUD-ZUID & OUD-WEST

Elegant homes and stylish shops, the Concertgebouw (Concert Hall) and world-famous museums: in many ways the Oud-Zuid is Amsterdam's most prosperous quarter, but the Oud-West comes a close second with its wonderful interior design stores and restaurants.

DISTRICT 5: REMBRANDTPLEIN, UTRECHTSESTRAAT & DE PIJP

Explore the Rembrantplein with its countless bars and open-air cafés, the shops and museums around Utrechtsestraat, the Amstel and Carré, then visit the trendy and multicultural district De Pijp: Amsterdam's answer to Notting Hill.

DISTRICT 6: EILANDEN

This used to be the eastern dock area, now you come to admire the modern and classic architecture of the warehouses and harbour buildings. Get some fresh air and watch the boats with a drink and a snack by the water. Last but not least there's the brand new Hermitage.

100% AMSTERDAM

Although Amsterdam's traditional motto reads 'heroic, resolute, charitable', this could very well be changed to 'fun, amazing and multicultural'. There's always something going on in 'Mokum' (a Dutch nickname for Amsterdam). But where do you start and what do you do? Shopping, a dose of culture, or delicious food? Amsterdam offers unique shops in the Negen Straatjes, modern architecture in the Eilanden, the best travel book store in the Oud-Zuid and the city's best ice cream in De Pijp. There are trendy restaurants, lively clubs, and the traditional brown cafés. This guide will make sure you don't miss a thing. Whether it's sightseeing, shopping, culinary delights or fun, the comprehensive maps will show you how to get there.

100% AMSTERDAM, DISCOVER THE CITY IN NO TIME!

Contents

About 100% Amsterdam

To make this guide easy to use, we divided Amsterdam into six interesting districts and provided each with its own detailed map. At the front, you'll find a comprehensive map that shows where the districts are in relation to each other. Using the letters (A) to (X), we have indicated where you can find the hotels, general places of interest and fun things to do, all described in detail further on in the guide.

In the following six chapters, you will find detailed descriptions of what to do in each district, the most important places of interest and the places for the best food and drink, shopping, relaxation and fun. Each address shows a number (1) that refers back to the map at the end of each district's chapter. The colour of each number indicates what you will find at each address:

● Places of interest	● Shopping
● Food & drinks	● Fun things to do

SIX WALKS

Each chapter includes a walk which takes about three hours, not including the time spent at places along the way. A line on the map indicates the route and you'll find a description of the walk on the opposite page. This will automatically guide you past the most interesting places and best addresses in each district, to ensure that you don't miss a thing. You will find places of interest, museums and parks as well as specialist shops, good places to lunch and the best restaurants for an evening meal. Those who don't want to follow the route can still use the descriptions and maps to discover the city their way.

INDICATION OF PRICES FOR HOTELS AND RESTAURANTS

To give you an idea of the prices of hotels and restaurants, we have included a price indication for each address. Unless otherwise stated, hotel prices are for a double room per night. It's worth checking out the prices of more expensive hotels on their websites, as they often have special offers. The prices shown for restaurants give an indication of the average price for a main meal, unless otherwise stated.

NATIONAL HOLIDAYS

As well as the flexible holidays for Easter, Ascension Day and Whitsun, the Netherlands has the following official holidays:

1st of January	- New Year's Day
30th of April	- Koninginnedag
25th & 26th of December	- Christmas

FESTIVALS

You can enjoy various annual festivals all over Amsterdam, mostly in the summer months. The following is a selection of the largest festivals:

Amsterdam Roots *(www.amsterdamroots.nl)*

Festival of global music, June, in the Oosterpark among other places.

Over het IJ Festival *(www.overhetij.nl)*

Theatre in Amsterdam-North, July, NDSM-shipyard.

Holland Festival *(www.hollandfestival.nl)*

Experimental music, opera, theatre and dance, May and June, Stadsschouwburg among other places.

Theater Amsterdamse Bos *(www.bostheater.nl)*

Open-air theatre, July and August, Amsterdamse Bos (Forest).

Kwakoe Festival *(www.kwakoefestival.com)*

Multicultural festival, six weekends in July and August, Bijlmerpark.

Gay Pride Parade ***(www.amsterdampride.nl)***
Extravagant parade on the canals, beginning of August, among others on the Prinsengracht.

De Parade ***(www.deparade.nl)***
Travelling theatre festival, first two weeks of August, Martin Luther Kingpark.

Grachtenfestival ***(www.grachtenfestival.nl)***
Classical music concerts, many are free. From June to August in the Vondelpark.

Uitmarkt ***(www.uitmarkt.nl)***
Opening of the cultural season, last weekend in August, among other places at the Leidseplein and Museumplein.

IDFA ***(www.idfa.nl)***
International documentary festival, November, in De Balie et al.

Hartjesdagen ***(www.hartjesdagen.nl)***
Small festival with plenty of folk singing, street acts and operetta, and its transvestite 'Hartjesparade' finale in August, on and around the Zeedijk.

Open-air theatre Vondelpark ***(www.openluchttheater.nl)***
A variety of free theatre acts, from June to August in the Vondelpark.

DO YOU HAVE ANY TIPS?

We have taken the greatest care in collecting the information for this guide, but shops and restaurants in Amsterdam constantly change. If you can't find the places you're looking for, or if you have any comments and/or tips for the guide, then please let us know via *www.100procentamsterdam.nl*. This site also gives you all the updates for and supplements to this guide and the events in the city.

For the record we should state that none of the recommended addresses paid for their entries, either for the text or for the photos. The entire text was written by objective editors.

Hotels

Amsterdam offers something for every taste and that also goes for its hotels. The hundreds of addresses give you a huge choice. Are you looking for something modern or would you rather go for traditional? Large or small? The prices vary from € 23.50 for a bed in a youth hostel to sky-high prices in a five-star hotel. Alongside the well-known chains and many medium-priced hotels, Amsterdam also offers some rather more unusual places to stay. You can find more information on the internet, and tracking down the attractive offers is really well worth the trouble.

www.expedia.nl or *www.booking.com* are the websites where you can find hotels to suit every budget. *www.sfeerhotels.nl* lists some very special hotels in hotels in Amsterdam.

www.amsterdam-accommodation.nl is handy if you want an apartment or just need bed & breakfast. *www.amsterdamtourist.nl* is the site for the Tourist Bureau in Amsterdam and it has information about the city, including hotels and other types of accommodation.

Below, we have listed some unusual hotels in various price ranges. They are each given a letter so that you can easily find them on the main map at the front of the guide. Unless otherwise stated, the price shown is for a double room without breakfast.

BUDGET

Ⓐ Tucked away among the rather dingy hotels in the Warmoesstraat, the **Winston** hotel comes as a nice surprise. This imaginative hotel is all about art. Eight of its 67 rooms have been designed by artists, the 'Heineken room' being the most popular. Its own nightclub, Winston Kingdom, is a real hotspot with live music.
warmoesstraat 129, telephone (0031) 020 623 13 80, www.winston.nl, price € 75, trams 1, 2, 4, 5, 9, 13, 14, 16, 17, 24, 25 dam

HOTEL ARENA (G)

(B) At the **Bickersbed**, you will be staying among the locals. These well-appointed studios are in a 17th century building on Bickerseiland, surrounded by Amsterdammers. During the Golden Age, this was the centre for global trade, but nowadays it's more like a village, with its narrow streets. The Bickersbed's studios are self-catering and each one is fitted with a fully-equipped kitchen.
grote bickersstraat 23 hs, telephone (0031) 020 422 82 64, www.bickersbed.nl, price € 80, city bus 18, 21, 22, from outside oranjestraat

(C) If you want something completely different, you could spend the night on a boat on the Amstel. The **Amstel Botel** offers 175 comfortable single, double and three-person rooms all en suite. Have you stayed here before? Please note: the botel has moved to the NDSM pier. The free ferry from Central Station takes you there in ten minutes.
NDSM pier 3, telephone (0031) 020 521 03 50, www.amstelbotel.nl, price € 89, Ferry behind Central Station, buses 91 & 94 from klaprozenweg

MID-RANGE

(D) Fancy staying somewhere where you can find the most scrumptious cakes literally on your doorstep? Then book a room at **Cake under my Pillow**, situated above the famous cake shop De Taart van m'n Tante (Aunty's Cake). You can choose from the white (quiet) room, green room (wonderful bathroom) or blue room (this is the loveliest with its Delft Blue tiles on the wall). For a slice of delicious cake you just wander downstairs.
eerste jacob van campenstraat 66, telephone (0031) 020 751 09 36, www.cakeundermypillow.com, price € 110, trams 16, 24, stadhouderskade

(E) In a quiet neighbourhood near the Vondelpark you'll find **De Filosoof** hotel with its large garden, bar and 38 rooms. Each room is unique and decorated with pearls of wisdom from famous philosophers. The Confucius room for instance, with its deep purple colours and light furniture, is dedicated to the Chinese philosophy of Confucius and Taoism. Here, you'll also find Spinoza, Nietzsche, and Wittgenstein, and themes including passion, clouds and water.
anna van den vondelstraat 6, telephone (0031) 020 683 30 13, www.hoteldefilosoof.nl, price € 105, tram 1, jan pieter heijestraat

Ⓕ On the Oostelijke Handelskade you will find the **Lloyd Hotel** in a lovingly restored national monument. This is a very special hotel with 120 rooms, varying in luxury from one to five stars. Fifty artists and designers have worked together to make each room unique. It also has a restaurant/lobby, which provides both quick snacks and complete meals, and a Cultural Embassy where you can enjoy readings, concerts, films and a library.
oostelijke handelskade 34, telephone (0031) 020 561 36 36, www.lloydhotel.com, price € 110, bus 43 lloydplein, tram 10 azartplein

Ⓖ **Hotel Arena** is still one of the city's most extraordinary hotels. This historic building is not just a trendy base for travellers but is also a popular dance mecca for many Amsterdammers. Saturday and Sunday nights are when it's all happening in the Arena Tonight's former chapel. The 121 hotel rooms are minimalistic in design. It has its own car park (€ 12 per 24 hours).
's-gravesandestraat 51, telephone (0031) 020 850 24 10, www.hotelarena.nl, price from € 109, tram 3 beukenweg, 7, 10 korte 's-gravesandestraat & 9, 14 mauritskade

TOP END

Ⓗ **Hotel V's** two sites provide everything you want of a budget boutique hotel. You can enjoy their free Wi-Fi, Apple computers and sleek design. One of the hotels is on the outskirts of De Pijp on the Victorieplein and the newest site is closer to the centre on the Frederiksplein.
victorieplein 42 & weteringschans 136, telephone (0031) 020 305 74 70 & 020 662 32 33, www.hotelv.nl, price € 130, trams 4, 12, 25 victorieplein & trams 4, 7, 10 weteringschans

Ⓘ Staying in Amsterdam longer? Then try the **Miauw Suites**. This is a concept hotel with two deluxe rooms and several suites with spectacular views over the Keizersgracht. The suites have fully equipped kitchens with SMEG equipment and free Wi-Fi internet. Absolutely ideal for a longer stay. The Negen Straatjes are right around the corner so you can enjoy the countless restaurants, boutiques and cafés.
hartenstraat 36, telephone (0031) 020 893 29 33, www.miauw.com, price from € 145, trams 1, 2, 4, 5, 9, 13, 14, 16, 17, 24, 25 dam

Ⓕ **LLOYD HOTEL**

(J) **Het Prinsenhuis** makes a wonderful alternative to a hotel room. Every apartment (there are three in total) has its own ambience: warm red, fresh green and fruity orange. They are designed with flair, and come with a balcony or patio.
prinsengracht 967, telephone (0031) 020 521 06 10, www.prinsenhuis.nl, price from € 165, tram 4 prinsengracht

(K) **The College Hotel** is a must for the discerning visitor. Situated in a 19th century schoolhouse, this hotel provides a first-rate service. It has a beautiful terrace and the local yuppies love to be seen in the trendy bar. The College Hotel's restaurant has a great reputation too.
roelof hartstraat 1, telephone (0031) 020 571 15 11, www.thecollegehotel.com, prices from € 175, tram 2, 3, 5, 12 roelof hartplein

(L) Since 1902, the city's unadulterated classic, the **American Hotel** (pronounced 'Américain'), has been renowned for its excellent service and beautiful rooms . The hotel has had a facelift and has a large terrace overlooking the Leidseplein. Amsterdammers still find the lovely art deco café-restaurant a perfect spot for reading, having a snack or enjoying Sunday brunch. Very popular with pop stars!
leidsekade 97, telephone (0031) 020 556 30 00, www.amsterdamamerican.nl, price € 200, trams 1, 2, 5, 7, 10 leidseplein

Transport

The easiest way to get to Amsterdam is by **train**. From the Centraal Station – which is being renovated because a new metro line is due to open in 2012 – you can walk into town in minutes. If you have to come by car, it's best to park in the so-called **P+R**, which stands for Park and Ride. The idea is that you leave the car at the Amsterdam Arena stadium, Sloterdijk train station, the Zeeburgereiland or the Olympic stadium, and switch to public transport. It costs € 6 for 24 hours (with a maximum of 96 hours) and this also includes two return tickets for public transport. This is much cheaper than parking in the city centre, where you have to pay up to € 4 per hour from 9 am to midnight. There is more information about the regulations on *www.parkerenamsterdam.nl.*

In the city centre, the safest place to leave your car is in a **parking garage**. Prices can be as much as € 4 per hour. The costs for **street parking** vary according to the area and can be anything from € 1.30 to € 4 per hour. A good rule of thumb is: the closer to the centre, the more expensive it will be. You can also buy a day ticket or a weekly ticket at any Stadstoezicht (City Surveillance) service point. These tickets are valid throughout the city.

Travelling in the city is easiest by **tram**. Amsterdam has sixteen tram lines, most of which go from the Centraal Station to the East, South and West districts of the city. Line 26 goes from Amsterdam Centraal Station towards the Oostelijke Eilanden and IJburg. The other tram routes connect the city areas.

The **bus** is handy for getting from the Centraal Station to areas of the city a bit further away from the centre, like Amsterdam Noord.

The **metro lines** 53 and 54 take you from the Centraal Station to Amsterdam Zuidoost (Southeast). Line 51 runs from the Centraal Station to Amstelveen via Buitenveldert and line 50 takes you from Amsterdam Sloterdijk station to Gein, via station Zuid. **Night buses** run all night via or from the Centraal Station. Go to *www.gvb.nl* for up to date information.

For **public transport**, the bus and tram cards have been replaced by the OV chip card (PT smart card). There are three types: personal, anonymous and disposable. You can use them in trams, buses and in the metro. The personal and anynomous chip cards have to be credited first. Don't forget to check in and out. For more information and prices, go to *www.ov-chipkaart.nl.*

You can hail a **taxi** in the street and there are also plenty of taxi ranks in the city. The telephone number for best-known taxi service, TCA, is *(0031)* 020 777 77 77. The maximum rate for a taxi with a maximum of four passengers is calculated using a start rate of € 7.50 (which includes the first two kilometres) and then a maximum of € 2.20 per kilometre after that. Always ask what the journey is going to cost before you set off and make sure that the driver has switched on his meter. The taxi rank at Amsterdam CS has recently been cleaned up so that it is now quite safe to get a taxi here.

One of the nicest ways of getting round the inner city is by the **hop on, hop off Canal Bus**. This boat sails through Amsterdam's canals along three routes with fourteen stops, all of which are convenient for the most popular museums, shopping districts and tourist sights. You can buy a day ticket (€ 20, valid till 12.00 the next day!) which allows you to get on and off along all three routes. While on board you will hear a running commentary about Amsterdam. See *www.canal.nl.* for more information. You can also take a **canal tour** along the Rokin. Or see the city by **bike**. There are plenty of hire companies in the city. Some websites are *www.bikes.nl, www.macbike.nl* and *www.bikecity.nl.* A new transport idea is the **bike taxis** that you will find primarily in the centre - ideal for those short hops. They cost € 1 for three minutes per person. You will also find genuine **tuktuks** here and there! You can book one of these marvels from Thailand and India via 0900 993 33 99.

City centre

Historic, cosmopolitan and red

Amsterdam how it is known best – you can feel this beautiful city's historic soul in the centre: how it all began, the transformations, the sheer opulence. This is where you'll find the oldest canals and churches and where you can still feel the attraction that draws in tourists from all over the world. Stately homes stand cheek by jowl with the world-famous red light district. The streets surrounding the Oude Kerk (Old Church) form the oldest part of the inner city. They date from the Middle Ages, when the city was still powered by the beer and herring trade.

The Golden Age changed all that. Impressive buildings with enormous indoor gardens were built all around the ring of canals, and the Kalverstraat was transformed from a dusty cattle market into a 'chic' shopping street. The most dynamic area is Chinatown and the Nieuwmarkt. The Zeedijk is crammed with the Asiatic shops and eateries, so popular with people from

1

all cultures. Don't be put off by the hoards of (drunken) tourists staggering around, there's more than enough to enjoy. You must try the boat trips on the canals, the theatres on the Nes and the myriad shops.

Don't miss the Dam with its National Monument, the Nieuwe Kerk where Princess Máxima and Crown Prince Willem-Alexander were married, and the Royal Palace. This was built in the 17th century as the town hall, but was offered as a palace to King Louis Napoleon at the start of the 19th century. It recently had a make-over and was restored to its former glory.

6 things not to be missed!

Royal Palace

Visit the Palace on the Dam

Puccini

Stock up on spicy pepper chocolates.

Oudemanhuispoort

Stroll through the gate among the students

Wallen

An evening stroll

Café Bern

Enjoy its famous cheese fondue.

Comedy Theater

Have a great evening out

- **Places of interest**
- **Shopping**
- **Food & drinks**
- **Fun things to do**

Places of interest

(4) The **National Monument on the Dam** was built in 1956 in memory of all the Dutch people who lost their lives during the Second World War. You can read the text written by the poet A. Roland Holst on the semi-circular memorial wall behind the obelisk.
dam, trams 1, 2, 4, 5, 9, 13, 14, 16, 24, 25 dam

(5) **Amsterdam's Royal Place** is still in frequent use during official celebrations. After its renovation in 2008, the Palace was partially reopened to the public. The building is austere and plain from the outside, but inside it is stunning with its restored chandeliers, furniture and masterpieces.
dam 1, telephone (0031) 020 620 40 60, www.paleisamsterdam.nl, open june-aug 11.00-17.00 & sep-may 12.00-17.00 (closed mondays), admission adult € 7.50, children 5-16 years € 6.50, trams 1, 2, 4, 5, 9, 13, 14, 16, 17, 24, 25 dam

(6) The **Nieuwe Kerk** (New Church) was built at the end of the 14th century to be the second church to the Oude Kerk (Old Church). You can enjoy its many major art and photo exhibitions, and see where Crown Prince Willem-Alexander and Princess Máxima were married on 2-2-2002.
gravenstraat 17, telephone (0031) 020 638 69 09, www.nieuwekerk.nl, limited opening times (only during exhibitions), admission variable, trams 1, 2, 4, 5, 9, 13, 14, 16, 17, 24, 25 dam

(11) The **Oudemanhuispoort** is a covered passageway that runs from the Oudezijds Achterburgwal to the Kloveniersburgwal. The gateway no longer leads to the Oudemannen- en Vrouwengasthuis (a former old peoples' home), but to Amsterdam University's main buildings. As well as hordes of students, you'll also find dozens of second-hand book and magazine stalls.
oudemanhuispoort, open mon-sat 12.00-18.00, trams 4, 9, 14, 16, 24, 25 muntplein

(15) A visit to the **Rembrandthuis** will give you a good idea how the famous artist lived and worked between 1639 and 1658. In one part of the museum you can see his paintings, etchings and sketches.
jodenbreestraat 4, telephone (0031) 020 520 04 00, www.rembrandthuis.nl, open daily 10.00-17.00, admission adults € 12, children 6-15 years € 1.50, trams 9, 14, metro 51, 53, 54 waterlooplein

(27) The **Fo Guang Shan He Hua Temple** is the largest Chinese-Buddhist temple in Europe. It's used for Buddhist celebrations and you can follow courses in Chinese or Buddhism. You can also take a guided tour any day except Sunday (book beforehand, though). *zeedijk 106-118, telephone (0031) 020 420 23 57, www.ibps.nl, open tues-sat 12.00-17.00, sunday 10.00-17.00, free, trams 1, 2, 4, 5, 9, 13, 16, 17, 24, 25, 26 centraal station*

(33) Hidden away in the attic of this canal house you will discover a 16th century church. In those days, the official churches were Reformed. Non-reformed churches could only hold services in places that weren't recognised as churches. This is how **Ons' Lieve Heer op Solder** came into being.
oudezijds voorburgwal 40, telephone (0031) 020 624 66 04, www.museumamstelkring.nl, open mon-sat 10.00-17.00, sunday and holidays 13.00-17.00, admission adults € 7, children 5-18 years € 1, 0-4 years free, trams 1 2, 4, 5, 9, 13, 16, 17, 24, 25 centraal station

(34) The **Oude Kerk** is Amsterdam's oldest monument and has now been given the status of a European Monument. On a regular basis, there are exhibitions and concerts in the Oude Kerk.
oudekerksplein 23, telephone (0031) 020 625 82 84, www.oudekerk.nl, open mon-sat 11.00-17.00, sunday 13.00-17.00, admission € 5, trams 1, 2, 4, 5, 9, 13, 16, 17, 24, 25

NATIONAL MONUMENT ON THE DAM (4)

Food & drinks

(2) Visit the **De Bakkerswinkel** and enjoy a healthy breakfast or lunch with delicious sandwiches of your own choice. Or enjoy the tasty pies, cakes and scones. Part of the cosy decor is by furniture designer Piet Hein Eek.
warmoesstraat 69, telephone (0031) 020 489 80 00, www.bakkerswinkel.nl, open tues-sunday 8.00-16.00, price € 12, trams 1, 2, 4, 5, 9, 13, 16, 17, 24, 25 centraal station

(10) You will find **Kapitein Zeppos** café-restaurant hidden away in the Gebed zonder End alley, where you can enjoy a drink, lunch and dinner in a homely atmosphere. It is in a nicely tucked away location, and it has live music on Sundays.
gebed zonder end 5, telephone (0031) 020 624 20 57, www.zeppos.nl, open mon-thurs & sunday 12.00-1.00, fri &sat 12.00-3.00, price € 26, trams 1, 2, 4,5, 9, 14, 16, 24, 25 spui

(20) **Café Bern** on the Nieuwmarkt serves absolutely the best cheese fondue in Amsterdam. The entrecote, however, which you can cook yourself at the table, isn't far behind. Order both for maximum enjoyment - it's what most of the regulars do.
nieuwmarkt 9, telephone (0031) 020 622 00 34, open daily 18.00-0.00, price € 15, trams 1, 2, 4, 5, 9, 13, 16, 17, 24, 25, 26 centraal station, metro 51, 53, 54 nieuwmarkt

(21) A little piece of Havana in the middle of Amsterdam. **Café Cuba** is still a wonderful classic, spilling over with Latin-American *gusto*. This is where you'll find the best mojitos, old rums and swinging music. It's late before you know it...
nieuwmarkt 3, telephone (0031) 020 627 49 19, open sunday-thurs 12.00-1.00, fri-sat 12.00-3.00, price € 18, trams 1, 2, 4, 5, 9, 13, 16, 17, 24, 25, 26 centraal station, metro 51, 53, 54 nieuwmarkt

LATEI 26

(22) You'll find café-restaurant **In de Waag** in Amsterdam's oldest city gateway (1488). You can enjoy your lunch, a drink or dinner surrounded by one metre thick walls, built in the Middle Ages and lit by three hundred candles. Alternatively, you can eat outside on the large terrace.
nieuwmarkt 4, telephone (0031) 020 422 77 72, www.indewaag.nl, open daily 10.00-1.00, price € 34, trams 1, 2, 4, 5, 9, 13, 16, 17, 24, 25, 26 centraal station, metro 51, 53, 54 nieuwmarkt

(23) Are you near the Nieuwmarkt and don't fancy Chinese or Thai food, but still want something good and cheap? Then you can't beat **Eetcafé van Beeren** with its 'bruine kroeg' (old-style pub) atmosphere and its steak and chips.
koningsstraat 54, telephone (0031) 020 622 23 29, open daily from 17.30, price € 22, trams 1, 2, 4, 5, 9, 13, 16, 17, 24, 25, 26 centraal station

(25) **Looks Dining** is certainly eye-catching and trendy but also offers a good quality and reasonably priced food. The weekly menu changes but the oysters and entrecote are always on offer. Perfect for that special celebration.
binnen bantammerstraat 5-7, telephone (0031) 020 320 09 49, www.restaurantlooks.nl, open mon-sat 18.00-1.00, price € 36, trams 1, 2, 4, 5, 9, 13, 16, 17, 24, 25 centraal station

(26) You would expect to see **Latei** in De Pijp or the Jordaan, but not in the red light district in between Chinese restaurants. So keep your eyes open, otherwise you'll miss it and that would be a shame. Besides getting a very good cup of coffee, you can also browse through memorabilia from the 1960s and 1970s. Everything you see is for sale, even the chair you're sitting on.
zeedijk 143, telephone (0031) 020 625 74 85, www.latei.net, price € 4, open mon-wed 8.00-18.00, thurs-fri. 8.00-22.00,sat 9.00-22.00, sunday 11.00-18.00, trams 1, 2, 4, 5, 9, 13, 16, 17, 24, 25, centraal station, metro 51, 53, 54 nieuwmarkt

(28) **Nam Kee** features in the book 'De oesters van Nam Kee' by Kees van Beijnum, which was made into a film starring Dutch actress Katja Schuurman. Nam Kee is famous for its good, reasonably priced and authentic Chinese food served in disconcertingly bright fluorescent lighting.
zeedijk 111, telephone (0031) 020 624 34 70, www.namkee.nl, open daily 12.00-23.00, price € 12, tram 1, 2, 4, 5, 9, 13, 16, 17, 24, 25, 26 centraal station

BRASSERIE HARKEMA (36)

(29) You won't believe how fast they can serve up the tastiest Thai dishes at **Snackbar Bird**. This tiny, popular snack bar is often chock-a-block. If you want to take your time, you're better off at the Bird Thais Restaurant over the road.
zeedijk 72-74, telephone snackbar (0031) 020 420 62 89, restaurant (0031) 020 620 14 42, www.thai-bird.nl, open snackbar daily 14.00-22.00, restaurant open daily 17.00-23.00, price € 17, trams 1, 2, 4, 5, 9, 13, 16, 17, 24, 25, 26 centraal station

(30) Wijs & Zonen have been selling their own blends of wonderful coffees and teas for years, and the ultimate place to drink them is the **Hofje van Wijs**; a genuine establisment on the Zeedijk. It's also the perfect place to have a sumptuous high tea with scones and delicious sandwiches.
zeedijk 43, telephone (0031) 020 624 04 36, www.wijs-zonen.nl, open tues-wed & sunday 12.00-18.00, thurs-fri 12.00-22.30, sat 10.00-22.30, price € 15, trams 1, 2, 4, 5, 9, 13, 16, 17, 24, 25, 26 centraal station

(31) Soak up the Old Amsterdam atmosphere in café **In 't Aepjen** . 'Aepjen' means 'monkey' and when this was a sailor's lodging house in the 15th century, any guest who couldn't pay his bill would have to bring back a monkey from his next voyage instead. The animals were crawling with fleas, and if people saw someone scratching frantically on the Zeedijk, they would say 'he's been staying at the Aep'.
zeedijk 1, telephone (0031) 020 626 84 01, open mon-thurs & sat 15.00-1.00, fri-sat 15.00-3.00, price € 3, trams 1, 2, 4, 5, 9, 13, 16, 17, 24, 25 centraal station

(36) **Brasserie Harkema** suprises you with its large open area, high ceilings and slick design. The huge wine rack and rainbow-coloured wall will certainly make an impact. Harkema is perfect for lunch or for a snack before going to a show at one of the nearby theatres.
nes 67, telephone (0031) 020 428 22 22, www.brasserieharkema.nl, open daily 11.00-1.00, price € 23, trams 1, 2, 4, 5, 9, 14, 16, 24, 25 spui

10

2

22

Shopping

(1) **Geels & Co** is, besides being a lovely store where you can buy various blends of tea and freshly ground coffee and coffee beans, also a (small) museum where you can learn everything about coffee and tea.
warmoesstraat 67, telephone (0031) 020 624 06 83, www.geels.nl, shop open mon-sat 9.30-18.00, sunday 13.00-17.00, museum open sat 14.00-16.30, trams 1, 2, 4, 5, 9, 13, 16, 17, 24, 25, 26 centraal station

(7) **SPR Specials** is the outlet for SPRMRKT on the Rozengracht. The collection changes every four to six months. An absolute must for men's and women's fashion, including Acne, Damir Doma and 7d.
nieuwezijds voorburgwal 262, no telephone, www.sprkmrkt.nl, open mon-tues & sunday 12.00-18.00, wed & sat 12.00-19.00, thurs-fri 12.00-20.00, trams 1, 2, 4, 5, 9, 13, 14, 16, 17, 24, 25 dam

(8) Do you love fairy tales? At **De Sprookjeskamer**, you'll find that Bambi, Heidi and red and white dots (toadstools) are still in. A place for bathrobes, dancing shoes, lampshades and all kinds of lovely things for (mostly) little girls.
nieuwezijds voorburgwal 383, telephone (0031) 020 420 00 15, www.desprookjeskamer.nl, open tues-sat 11.00-17.30, trams 1, 2, 4, 5, 9, 14, 16, 24, 25 spui

(9) **P.G.C. Hajenius** still cossets smokers, and provides excellent service and the very best tobacco products from all over the world. It's no wonder that they have been supplying European royal houses for so many years. Non-smokers will also find this national monument well worth a visit.
rokin 96, telephone (0031)020 623 74 94, www.hajenius.com, open mon 12.00-18.00, tues-sat 9.30-18.00, sunday 12.00-17.00, trams 1, 2, 4, 5, 9, 14, 16, 24, 25 spui

(12) Dutch Design has conquered the world, and **Droog Design** played an important part in that process. In the shop/showroom you will find worldfamous Dutch designers to suit large and small budgets.
staalstraat 7b, telephone (0031) 020 523 50 59, www.droog.com, open tues-sat 12.00-18.00, trams 4, 9, 14, 16, 24, 25 muntplein

16

8

⑲ **2PR**

⑬ Wickedly delicious chocolates, or rather...'bomboni' , that's what you'll find at **Puccini**. Traditionally, they are bonbons with caramel or marzipan, but here they are also combined with lemon grass or pepper. Be careful: highly addictive. *staalstraat 17, telephone (0031) 020 626 54 74, www.puccinibomboni.com, open mon & sunday 12.00-18.00, tues-sat 9.00-18.00, trams 4, 9, 14, 16, 24, 25 muntplein*

⑭ Just behind the Stadhuis (Town Hall) and the Muziektheater (Music Theatre) is the **Waterlooplein** with no less than three hundred small stalls selling mostly second hand goods. Nowadays, it isn't as cheap anymore, but it is still fun to visit. *waterlooplein, www.waterloopleinmarkt.nl, open mon-sat 10.00-17.00, trams 9, 14, metro 51, 53, 54 waterlooplein*

(16) **Bis** is actually three vintage shops in a row. Number 25a specializes in army- and sports clothing, both foreign and domestic. 25b is their shoe shop, selling bags, hats and accessories. At 25d you can go mad buying clothes from the 1950s to the 1990s.
sint antoniesbreestraat 25a, 25b, 25d, telephone (0031) 020 620 34 67, www.bis-vintage.nl, open mon-sat 11.00-18.00, trams 9, 14, metro 51, 53, 54 waterlooplein

(17) At **Zipper** you can rummage through shelves and baskets full of second-hand clothes. Blouses from the Fifties and Sixties, glittery jackets, bell-bottom trousers, miniskirts, belts, boots and oh so much more.
nieuwe hoogstraat 10, telephone (0031) 020 627 03 53, www.zipperstore.nl, open mon 12.00-18.00, tues-wed & fri-sat 11.00-18.00, thurs 11.00-21.00, sunday 13.00-17.00, trams 1, 2, 4, 5, 9, 13, 14, 16, 17, 24, 25 dam

(18) **Puck** is housed inside a lovely building; it's a romantic little shop with gorgeous second-hand dresses, blouses, hats, jewellery and other accessories. They also have a large collection of new clothes for women and children.
nieuwe hoogstraat 1, telephone (0031) 020 625 42 01, open mon 13.00-18.00, tues-sat 11.00-18.00, sunday 13.00-17.00, trams 1, 2, 4, 5, 9, 13, 14, 16, 17, 24, 25 dam

(19) Are you a man who wants to look good? Then visit **2PR**, for Hugo Boss, Drykorn, Acne, Swear: simplicity and quality at reasonable prices. 2PR recently opened a second, smaller branch at 12 Gasthuismolensteeg.
oude hoogstraat 10-12, telephone (0031) 020 421 34 99/63 29, www.2pr.eu, open mon & sunday 12.00-18.00, tues-wed & fri-sat 10.00-18.00, thurs 10.00-21.00, trams 1, 2, 4, 5, 9, 13, 14, 16, 17, 24, 25 dam

(35) If you're looking for really special footwear, then go to **Betsy Palmer**. This shop is simply packed with the cutest shoes. As well as their own label, they also have shoes by Tods, Bloom, Uggs and other designer labels.
rokin 9-15, telephone (0031) 020 422 10 40, www.betsypalmer.nl, open mon 12.30-18.30, tues-wed & fri 10.30-18.30, thurs 10.30-21.00, sat 10.00-18.00, sunday 13.00-18.00, trams 1, 2, 4, 5, 9, 13, 14, 16, 17, 24, 25 dam

Fun things to do

(3) All the more fun because it's so unexpected and different: **W139** in the Warmoesstraat. An exhibition hall of (inter)national fame and a haven for the visual arts. It is, in other words, a place where artists are given free rein to experiment. So step inside and marvel at the contemporary art projects.
warmoesstraat 139, telephone (0031) 020 622 94 34, www.w139.nl, free, open mon-sat 11.00-19.00, trams 1, 2, 4, 5, 9, 13, 14, 16, 17, 24, 25 dam

(24) Stroll along the city's lesser known canals and locks... Of course we all know about the Herengracht and the Prinsengracht, but the district surrounding the **Rechtboomsloot, Kromboomsloot** and the **Oude Schans** might well be one of the most beautiful in the city. You really shouldn't miss the Montelbaanstoren on the Oude Schans, an old defence tower dating from 1516. Where does its name come from? No one knows.
kromboomsloot, rechtboomsloot, oude schans, trams 1, 2, 4, 5, 9, 13, 14, 16, 17, 24, 25 dam

(32) Go for a walk on the **Wallen**. Stroll around the Oudezijds Achter- and Voorburgwal. Don't miss the Trompetsteeg, Amsterdam's smallest street, and Casa Rosso. Standing on the Stoofbrug at night, the views over the Wallen and all the many-coloured lights are very beautiful.
oudezijds voorburgwal en oudezijds achterburgwal, trams 1, 2, 4, 5, 9, 13, 16, 17, 24, 25, 16 centraal station

(37) A visit to the new **Comedy Theater** on the Nes is a must. This marvellous little cabaret and stand-up comedy theatre has built up a solid reputation very quickly, and you'll find famous and not-so-famous performers on stage. There is also a special childrens' cabaret.
nes 110, telephone (0031) 020 422 27 77, www.comedytheater.nl, admission and opening times vary, trams 1, 2, 4, 5, 9, 14, 16, 24, 25 spui, metro 51, 53, 54 nieuwmarkt

24

3

comedy
theater
in de
Nes
COMEDY THEATER
37

24

City Centre

WALK 1

Walk from the Central Station towards the Dam. Turn left just before the Beurs van Berlage and take the second street on the right into the Warmoesstraat 1 2 3. Walk on towards the Dam 4 5 6. Walk behind the Paleis op de Dam and turn left into the Nieuwezijds Voorburgwal past all the shops 7 8. At the end, turn left into the Spui. Cross over the Kalverstraat, the Rokin 9 and turn into the Lange Brugsteeg. Walk into the Gebed Zonder End alley 10 or follow the Grimburgwal until you come to the Oudemanhuispoort 11. Turn right under the gateway and cross over the bridge to the Staalstraat for the designer shops 12 or indulge your chocolate addiction 13. Carry on walking to the Waterlooplein 14. Walk towards the Jodenbreestraat for the Rembrandthuis 15 and stroll to the Antoniesbreestraat 16. Or you can turn immediately left into the Nieuwe Hoogstraat 17 18 19. When you reach the waterside of the Kloveniersburgwal canal, turn right towards the Nieuwmarkt 20 21 22. Walk along the Nieuwmarkt towards the Geldersekade and turn right into the Koningsstraat 23. Have a look around the Kromboomsloot 24 or turn left towards the Oude Waal, via the Binnen bantammerstraat 25 You are now heading back to the Nieuwmarkt via the Geldersekade. Cross the square. Turn right onto the Zeedijk 26 and enjoy a great welcome in Chinatown with its Buddhist temple 27. The Zeedijk is another world with its authentic Asian shops and restaurants, like the famous Nam Kee 28 and the Bird snackbar 29. But it isn't a totally Far East experience. You're back in Holland when you get to the Hofje van Wijs 30. At the end of the Zeedijk, you can see one of the only two wooden houses left in Amsterdam 31. Turn left into the Sint Olofspoort, and left again onto the Oudezijds Voorburgwal. You are now on the Wallen 32. At the top of the canalside house at number 46 there is a hidden church in the attic 33. The Oude Kerk is a little further along 34. If you want to see more of the Wallen, walk to the end of the Oudezijds Voorburgwal and Oudezijds Achterburgwal. Walk along the Oudezijds Voorburgwal then eventually turn right into the Damstraat, pop into the Betsy Palmer shoe shop 35 and then turn off into the Nes for a bite to eat 36 or an evening of stand-up comedy 37.

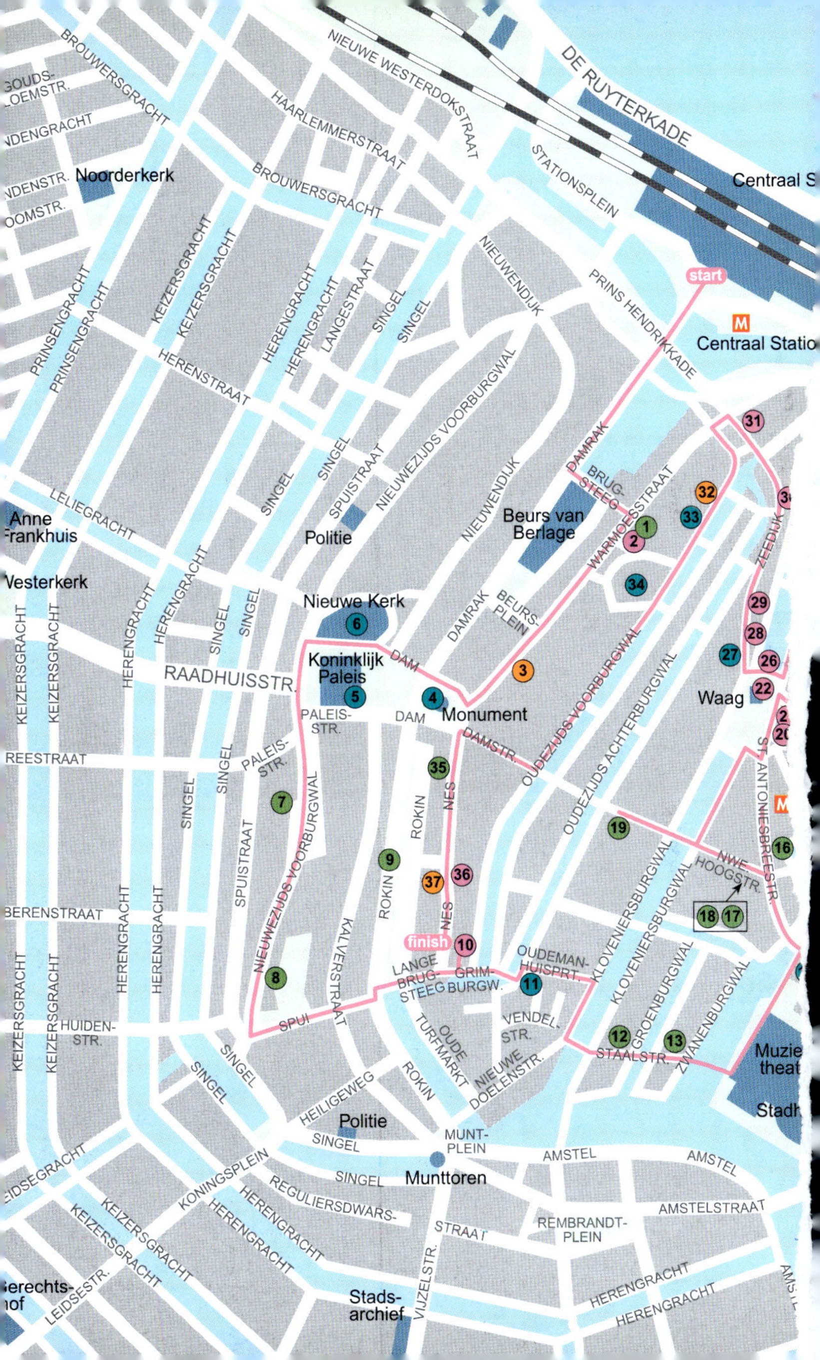

DE RUYTERKADE
Centraal S
Centraal Statio
start
finish
STATIONSPLEIN
PRINS HENDRIKKADE
NIEUWE WESTERDOKSTRAAT
BROUWERSGRACHT
HAARLEMMERSTRAAT
GOUDS-
LOEMSTR.
NDENGRACHT
NDENSTR.
OOMSTR.
Noorderkerk
PRINSENGRACHT
KEIZERSGRACHT
HERENGRACHT
LANGESTRAAT
SINGEL
HERENSTRAAT
NIEUWENDIJK
NIEUWEZIJDS VOORBURGWAL
SPUISTRAAT
LELIEGRACHT
Anne
Frankhuis
Westerkerk
Politie
DAMRAK
BRUG-
STEEG
WARMOESSTRAAT
Beurs van
Berlage
BEURS-
PLEIN
ZEEDIJK
Nieuwe Kerk
Koninklijk
Paleis
DAM
RAADHUISSTR.
Monument
PALEIS-
STR.
DAMSTR.
OUDEZIJDS VOORBURGWAL
OUDEZIJDS ACHTERBURGWAL
Waag
REESTRAAT
NES
ROKIN
KALVERSTRAAT
NWE.
HOOGSTR.
ST. ANTONIESBREESTR.
KLOVENIERSBURGWAL
GROENBURGWAL
ZWANENBURGWAL
BERENSTRAAT
LANGE
BRUG-
STEEG
GRIM-
BURGW.
OUDEMAN-
HUISPRT.
SPUI
HUIDEN-
STR.
VENDEL-
STR.
OUDE
TURFMARKT
NIEUWE
DOELENSTR.
STAALSTR.
Muzie
theat
Stadh
HEILIGEWEG
Politie
MUNT-
PLEIN
Munttoren
AMSTEL
AMSTELSTRAAT
REGULIERSDWARS-
STRAAT
REMBRANDT-
PLEIN
KONINGSPLEIN
LEIDSEGRACHT
LEIDSESTR.
VIJZELSTR.
Stads-
archief
erechts-
hof
1 2 3 4 5 6 7 8 9 10 11 12 13 16 17 18 19 20 22 26 27 28 29 31 32 33 34 35 36 37

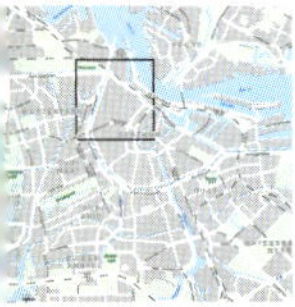

Jordaan

Amsterdam, bohemians, village-like and hip

It's still a mystery how the Jordan got its name. Some say it's a reference to the River Jordan, while others think that it's a corruption of the French word jardin meaning 'garden', as many of the streets are named after flowers. We'll probably never know.

But one thing we do know is that this is the place to find fascinating little shops, brown cafés and snack bars, and an abundance of charm. The small streets, canals and courtyards give the area its distinctive beauty. The Westerkerk proudly overlooks the houses and on the Prinsengracht, you can find the house where Anne Frank wrote her diary. The Brouwersgracht is perhaps the most romantic place in Amsterdam. Note that there are very few trams, buses and cars in this neighbourhood. The Jordaan feels rather like a village within Amsterdam.

2

The numerous traditional businesses that you used to find in the Jordaan have now disappeared, making way for shops and homes. One exception is the Van Wees gin distillery, better known as De Ooievaar in the Driehoekstraat. Nowadays you won't often come across the genuine 'Jordanese' with their distinctive dialect. In the 1970s, most of them left en masse for Lelystad, Almere or Purmerend.

Since then, there has been a huge rise in house prices and the Jordaan, originally built for the working classes, is now mostly inhabited by the rich. You'll mostly come across students with wealthy parents and yuppies with their cargo bikes, Bugaboos and dogs, plus hordes of tourists in the summer. In spite of these many changes in its population, however, the Jordaan is still the Jordaan: one of the most charming quarters in Amsterdam. One tip: take cash with you because oddly enough there aren't many cash dispensers there.

6 things not to be missed!

Noordermarkt

Visit the organic market on Saturday.

Anne Frank Huis

See where Anne Frank wrote her diary.

Papeneiland

Enjoy a nice glass of beer in this traditional 'bruine kroeg' (old-style pub).

Karthuizerhofje

Have a wander in one of the Jordaan courtyard gardens.

Kat in de Wijngaert

Try one of the best toasted sandwiches in town.

The Movies

Finish off with a film in the old art-deco cinema.

- Places of interest
- Shopping
- Food & drinks
- Fun things to do

Places of interest

(1) The **Westerkerk's** 85 metre-high tower is the icon of the Jordaan. On 10 March 1966, Princess Beatrix and Prince Claus solemnized their marriage in this 17th century edifice. The church is still in use and admission is free.
prinsengracht 281, telephone (0031) 020 624 77 66, www.westerkerk.nl, open april-oct mon-fri 11.00-15.00, july-aug mon-fri 11.00-15.00, sat 11.00-15.00, free, trams 13, 14, 17 westermarkt

(2) You can see Anne Frank and her family's hiding place at the world famous **Anne Frank Huis**. Her original diary is still on display. Try to visit out of season and as early as possible because the queues can be very long.
prinsengracht 267, telephone (0031) 020 556 71 00, www.annefrankhuis.nl, open sept-march 9.00-19.00, april-june 9.00-21.00, july & aug 9.00-22.00, admission adults € 8.50, children 10-17 years € 4, 0-9 years free, trams 13, 14, 17 westermarkt

(5) A treat for all the fans of much-loved Dutch author Theo Thijssen: the **Theo Thijssen Museum**. This is the house where the Amsterdam author, teacher, union official and politician was born and where his manuscripts, first editions, photos and visual and audio material are on display. You can also arrange to go for a walk through the Jordaan on request.
eerste leliedwarsstraat 16, telephone (0031) 020 420 71 19, www.theothijssenmuseum.nl, open thurs-sunday 12.00-17.00, admission € 2, trams 13, 14, 17 westermarkt

(16) The impressive **Noorderkerk** was built at the beginning of the 17th century to serve the northern part of the Jordaan, as the Westerkerk was deemed to be too far away. It is still used by the Dutch Reformed Church. You can find the Amsterdam Council's Archaeological Department in one of the annexes
noordermarkt 48, www.noorderkerk.org, open mon 10.30-15.00, sat 11.00-13.00, sunday 13.30-17.30, free, trams 13, 14, 17 westermarkt

33 LETTING

Food & drinks

(3) **Spanjer & Van Twist** is a friendly brown café-bar for lunches and dinners. The food is very reasonably priced. There is a long table full of reading material and in the summer the terrace on the canal is very popular.
leliegracht 60, telephone (0031) 020 639 01 09, www.spanjerenvantwist.nl, open daily 10.00-1.00, price € 21, trams 13, 14, 17 westermarkt

(4) At **De Reiger** you can enjoy a beer at the bar before you go to your table. The menu is simple with meals like steak and fried potatoes with salad.
nieuwe leliestraat 34, telephone (0031) 020 624 74 26, open mon-sat 11.00-1.00, sunday 11.00-0.00, price € 26, trams 13, 14, 17 westermarkt

(6) **Mantoe** is the first and only Afghan restaurant in Amsterdam. To give you an idea, the food is a little bit like Turkish and Indian cuisine, but don't expect a themed restaurant with Afghan hats on the ceiling and carpets on the wall. This is a modern eatery with an unusual cuisine, which is well worth a visit.
tweede leliedwarsstraat 13, telephone (0031) 020 421 63 74, www.restaurantmantoe.nl, price € 28, open wed-sunday 17.00-22.30, trams 13, 14, 17 westermarkt

(7) A great plus for **Café't Smalle** is its small terrace along the canal - perfect for a summer lunch overlooking all the little boats. Inside, this tiny place is just what you would expect if you were looking for a 'bruine kroeg' (traditional café). Its house wine is considered to be one of the best in town.
egelantiersgracht 12, telephone (0031) 020 623 96 17, www.t-smalle.nl, open sunday-thurs 10.00-1.00, fri-sat 10.00-2.00, price € 6, trams 13, 14, 17 westermarkt

(8) Don't even think about asking for syrup at the **Japanese Pancake World**. Japanese pancakes, called *okonomiyaki* , are not at all like the homely Dutch variety. They have a huge selection of fillings: from slices of beef and spring onions to shrimps and shiitake mushrooms. Delicious and different.
tweede egelantiersdwarsstraat 24a, telephone (0031) 020 320 44 47, www.japanesepancakeworld.com, open thurs, fri & sunday 18.00-22.00, sat 12.00-22.00, price € 14, trams 13, 14, 17 westermarkt

(11) Even though the **Cinema Paradiso** has a large open trattoria, it's always incredibly busy. The menu is Italian: antipasti, bruschetta, pizza or pasta, and as dessert you must try their famous drink, scroppino. You can't book a table, but there is an excellent bar where you can enjoy a drink while you are waiting.
westerstraat 184-186, telephone (0031) 020 623 73 44, www.cinemaparadiso.info, open wed-sunday 18.00-23.00, price € 25, trams 13, 14, 17 westermarkt

(13) **Kat in de Wijngaert** is well known as filmmaker Eddy Terstall's (Simon, Hufters & Hofdames) favourite local, and as that of a large part of his regular cast. Even if you've never heard of him, you'll still love the place. According to Amsterdam's newspaper Het Parool, they serve the best toasted sandwiches in town. Expect a typical Jordaan welcome and, naturally, a friendly café cat.
lindengracht 160, telephone (0031) 020 622 45 54, open mon-thurs & sunday 10.00-1.00, fri-sat10.00-2.00, price € 2, trams 13, 14, 17 westermarkt

(14) An evening in **Duende** tapas bar will never disappoint, unless you object to ordering your own snacks at the bar. The tapas are delicious and reasonably priced and the atmosphere is relaxed. You can't book a table.
lindengracht 62, telephone (0031) 020 420 66 92, www.cafe-duende.nl, open mon-thurs 16.00-1.00, fri 16.00-3.00, sat 12.00-3.00,sunday 14.00-1.00, price € 23, trams 13, 14, 17 westermarkt

(15) At **Eetcafé Koevoet**, based in a typical Amsterdam upstairs room, they will simply spoil you . A cosy, romantic and ever-so-slightly old fashioned restaurant where you will find really good food. Try the grilled catfish kebab, marinated veal escalope and surprisingly different pastas, with cat's paw parfait or chocolate mousse for dessert.
lindenstraat 17, telephone (0031) 020 624 08 46, open tues-sunday 18.00-22.00, price € 28, trams 13, 14, 17 westermarkt

(18) **Winkel 43** is a favourite spot for a snack and a drink in the heart of the Jordaan. Don't miss their delicious apple pie. In summertime, the long wooden outside tables are always packed. Sit yourself down, order a glass of rosé and you won't want to move again.
noordermarkt 43, telephone (0031) 020 623 02 23, open mon-thurs 8.00-0.00, fri-sat 8.00-3.00, price € 20, trams 13, 14, 17 westermarkt

(19) **19 Proust** can suddenly get really busy, especially on Friday afternoons. It's a really popular bar for a drink and a meal. If you pop in here on Mondays on your way back from the Noordermarkt, you can plonk yourself down with all your new goodies. The meals are simple and tasty.
noordermarkt 4, telephone (0031) 020 623 91 45, open tues-thurs & sunday 12.00-1.00, fri 12.00-3.00, sat 10.00-3.00, price € 19, trams 13, 14, 17 westermarkt

(20) **Papeneiland** is one of the oldest and most authentic 'bruine kroegen' (traditional cafés) in Amsterdam. It's a small bar inside a lovely historic building with Delft-blue tiles and a wood burning stove. There's no music, so make sure you have plenty to gossip about.
prinsengracht 2, telephone (0031) 020 624 19 89, www.papeneiland.nl, open mon 9.00-1.00, tues-thurs 10.00-1.00, fri 10.00-2.00, sat 9.00-2.00, sunday 12.00-1.00, price € 2.50, trams 13, 14, 17 westermarkt

(21) **Café Tabac** is located in one of the most beautiful spots in Amsterdam. It will remind you of the song 'On the Canals of Amsterdam'. You can relax outside on one of the cushions, pop inside for a drink or enjoy the simple cuisine which offers mostly Eastern dishes.
brouwersgracht 101, telephone (0031) 020 622 44 13, www.cafetabac.eu, open mon & sunday 11.00-1.00, tues-thurs 16.00-1.00, fri 16.00-3.00, sat 11.00-3.00, price € 2.50, tram 13, 14, 17 westermarkt

(30) Anyone who wants to experience a real Mokum night out has to make a stopoff at **Café Nol**. Drink in the atmosphere and the alcohol in this kitschy, typically Jordanese café where locals, students and other befuddled night owls warble along with André Hazes, Willy Alberti and others champions of the torch song. Make sure you arrive after midnight and are none too sober.
westerstraat 109, telephone (0031) 020 624 53 80, www.cafenolamsterdam.nl, open mon-thurs & sunday 21.00-3.00, fri-sat 21.00-4.00, price € 3, trams 13, 14, 17 westermarkt

(33) Taste what is probably the best cheesecake in Amsterdam in **Letting**, a small bar in the Prinsenstraat. Its customers tend to be a mix of lost tourists, freelancers with laptops and people coming from the Noordermarkt. Everything on the menu is available all day (including the cheesecake), but when it's gone, it's gone.
prinsenstraat 3, telephone (0031) 020 627 93 93, www.letting.nl, open daily 8.00-17.00, price € 4, trams 1, 2, 5, 13, 17 nieuwezijds kolk, tram 10 nassaukade

CAFÉ 'T SMALLE 7

㉒ RESTORED

Shopping

(9) You might just find that wonderful once-in-a-lifetime bargain at **De Kleedkamer.** Nearly-new Prada shoes, second hand Diesel jeans and beautiful, worn-only-once dresses. The window is full of gorgeous jewellery and chic hats. Sorry shopaholic men – they only sell women's clothes.
tweede egelantiersdwarsstraat 8, telephone (0031) 020 421 08 38, www.dekleedkamer.com, open mon & wed-sat 11.00-18.00, trams 13, 14, 17 westermarkt

(10) Are you looking for a vintage jumper or sixties' trousers? You can't do better than **Moriaan**, a shop chock-full of good quality, wearable second hand clothing.
tweede anjeliersdwarsstraat 19, telephone (0031) 020 620 47 98, open mon-fri 12.00-18.00, sat 11.00-18.00, trams 13, 14, 17 westermarkt

(22) **Restored** is one of those places that immediately inspire you. It's a shop, studio and workshop all in one, crammed with unique handmade accessories, fashion and interior items by artists and designers, i.e. just irresistible. You can also have a go yourself; Restored holds workshops for the creative souls among you, where you can work on your own projects. Email them for more information.
haarlemmerdijk 39, telephone (0031) 020 337 64 73, www.restored.nl, open mon-fri 10.00-18.00, sat 11.00-17.00, trams 1, 2, 5 13, 17 martelaarsgracht

(23) Welcome to this traditional candy heaven. In **Papabubble,** you can really indulge your sweet tooth. In this 'live sweet studio' they will make the most bizarre but delicious creations before your very eyes: giant lollies, sweets in every colour of the rainbow, or shaped like animals. For the more creative sugar addict.
haarlemmerdijk 70, telephone (0031) 020 626 26 62, www.papabubble.nl, open mon 12.00-18.00, tues-sat 10.00-18.00, tram 3 haarlemmerplein

(24) If you're looking for that perfect bag or purse then go to **Cellarrich**. Apart from their own collection of washable bags, made from suede, calfskin and leather, they also sell other brands. The table in the middle of the shop is covered with gorgeous jewellery and accessories.
haarlemmerdijk 98, telephone (0031) 020 626 55 26, www.cellarrich.nl, open mon-tues 13.00-18.00, wed-fri 11.00-18.00, sat 11.00-17.00, tram 3 haarlemmerplein

(25) The better art house films can't usually be found in the DVD rack at the Free Record Shop, but they do have them at the small, delightfully chaotic **The Silver Screen**. Here you'll find that DVD you've been looking for all these years, unique film posters and other memorabilia. An absolute must for every cinephile.
haarlemmerdijk 94, telephone (0031) 020 638 13 41, open tues-fri 12.30-18.00, sat 11.00-18.00, tram 3 haarlemmerplein

(26) The **Vivian Hann** shop is defined by its own style; aesthetics, simplicity and classiness are key. You'll find tableware by Dibbern, Rosenthal and Royal Copenhagen, German pottery by Pott and Japanese porcelain. There's also table linen by Margit Seland and lots of other lovely things.
haarlemmerdijk 102, telephone (0031) 06 220 494 65, open wed-fri 11.00-17.30,sat 10.30-17.00, tram 3 haarlemmerplein

(27) *Che bella!* **Ramona** is all about the latest Italian fashion shoes. This brilliant corner shop offers a limited but elegant selection of top quality shoes from Milan. You can also find some fabulous bags and accessories.
haarlemmerdijk 124, telephone (0031) 020 625 18 70, open mon 13.00-18.00, tues-fri 10.00-18.00, sat 10.00-17.30, tram 3 haarlemmerplein

(28) Grown-ups can nose around at **Teuntje** while the kids have fun playing with all the toys. Teuntje sells children's clothing in sizes 50 to140, shoes up to size 30, Bugaboo and Easy Walker strollers, and, of course, an abundance of wonderful toys!
haarlemmerdijk 132, telephone (0031) 020 625 34 32, www.teuntje.nu, open mon 13.00-18.00, tues-fri 10.00-18.00, sat 10.00-17.00, tram 3 haarlemmerplein

TEUNTJE 28

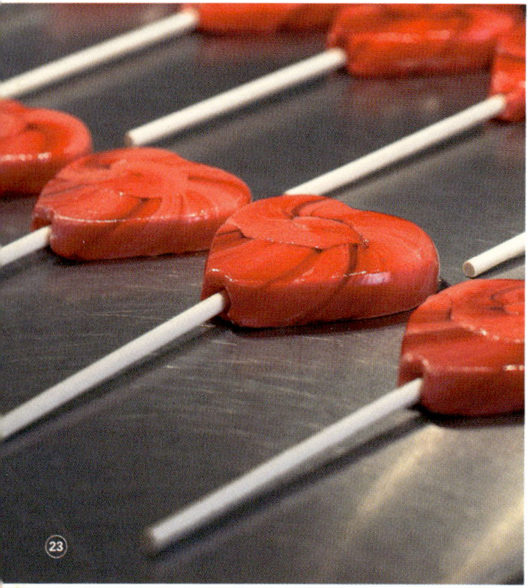
23

ANNO
31

(31) **Anno** sells furniture, lamps and other accessories from the 1950s to the 1980s, by famous and not-so-famous designers. The owner has a nose for beautiful things, from art deco to flower power and everything in between.
westerstraat 35-37, telephone (0031) 020 421 26 23, www.annodesign.nl, open mon 10.00-18.00, tues-fri 11.00-18.00, sat 10.00-17.00, trams 13, 14, 17 westermarkt

(32) **Margriet Nannings** not only sells her own women's clothing line but also labels including Paul Smith, Isabelle Marant and Girbeaud. In the men's shop, you'll find Comme des Garçons, Paul Smith, John Richmond and Victor Victoria. The outlet shop at number 15 stocks the old collections from both stores.
prinsenstraat 6, 8 & 15, telephone (0031) 020 420 20 97, www.margrietnannings.com, open mon 13.00-18.00, tues-wed & fri-sat 10.30-18.00, thurs 10.30-20.00, trams 13, 14, 17 westermarkt

(34) **Outras Coisas** is actually too small to house everything the owner wants to display. This little shop is crammed with out-of-the ordinary household goods and accessories: from bags to pottery that you won't come across anywhere else. You'll probably want to buy the lot.
herenstraat 31, telephone (0031) 020 625 72 81, open mon 12.00-18.00, tues-sat 11.00-18.00, sunday 12.00-17.00, trams 13, 14, 17 westermarkt

⑰ NOORDERMARKT

Fun things to do

(12) The Jordaan is famous for its numerous almshouses with inner gardens. You have to know where to find them because they're often hidden behind a nondescript door or gateway. Catching a glimpse behind one of these gateways is like looking through to another world; go though and you'll find yourself in a quiet green haven. The **Karthuizerhofje** dates from 1650 and was built for impoverished widows. Nowadays, the housing corporations let them out to private individuals
karthuizerstraat 21-131, tram 13, 14, 17 westermarkt

(17) To experience the authentic Jordanese ambience, you have to go to one of the markets. There's an organic famers' market on the **Noordermarkt** every Saturday, and a few stalls in the same square selling second-hand furniture and curiosa. You'll find fish, meat, vegetables, clothing and textiles on the Lindengracht, and on Monday mornings there's a fabrics market on the Noordermarkt.
noordermarkt, sat farmers' market 9.00-16.00, mon fabrics market 9.00-12.00, trams 13, 14, 17 westermarkt

(29) The oldest cinema in Amsterdam isn't Tuschinski, but **The Movies**. This film theatre dates from 1912. The beautiful art deco interior makes The Movies a stylish cinema where you can watch films in comfortable chairs. You will usually be able to view short (and better) films.
haarlemmerdijk 161-163, telefoon 020 624 57 90 (reserveringen vanaf 15.00), www.themovies.nl, entree volwassenen € 8,50-9,50, kinderen € 7, tram 3 haarlemmerplein

Jordaan

WALK 2

From the Westerkerk, (1) walk into the Jordaan via the Prinsengracht. You will see the Anne Frank House almost immediately (2). Directly over the bridge on your right you can have a coffee at Spanjer & Van Twist (3). Or turn left over the bridge and keep bearing left, then turn right and carry on down the left-hand side of the Egelantiersgracht. Turn off into the Nieuwe Leliestraat (4) and admire the view of the Westertoren from the Eerste and Tweede Leliedwarsstraat (5) (6). Turn back towards the Egelantiersgracht and walk on into 't Smalle (7), or turn off just before into the Tweede Egelantiersdwarsstraat (8) (9) and the Tweede Anjeliersdwarsstraat (10) for lots more super shops. Cross over the Westerstraat to the Cinema Paradiso (11). Walk into the Tichelstraat and turn right into the Karthuizerstraat (12). Turn left into the Tweede Lindendwarsstraat and then right into the Lindengracht for the best toasted sandwiches in the city (13) and first class tapas (14). Turn right into the Noorderkerkstraat. A bit further up on your right, there's a really good snack bar (15). Carry on till you come to the Noordermarkt (16) (17). Have lunch at Winkel 43 (18) on the corner of the Noordermarkt and the Westerstraat, or at one of the other cafés round the square (19). Carry on walking north over the Prinsengracht towards the bridge opposite Papeneiland (20). From here, or from the café on the opposite side, you have some wonderful views over the canal (21). From the Brouwersgracht, turn left and via the Korte Prinsengracht walk towards the Haarlemmerdijk for shopping (22) (23) (24) (25) (26) (27) (28). Pop into The Movies (29) to admire the lovely art-deco interior, then turn left at the Haarlemmerplein and via the Nieuwe Wagenstraat left again into the Brouwersgracht. Now cross the bridge over the Palmgracht and pay a visit to the Raepenhofje at 28-38. Turn left into the Palmdwarsstraat. Carry on along this street. If you want more shops and restaurants, then turn right into the Westerstraat (30) (31). Once you're back on the route, turn left at the end of the Violettenstraat into the Anjeliersstraat, and then turn right onto the Prinsengracht and cross the bridge. If you're up for more shopping, walk straight on into the Prinsenstraat (32) Finish off with a mouth-watering cheesecake at Letting (33). Or walk on a bit further to the Herenstraat for even more shops (34).

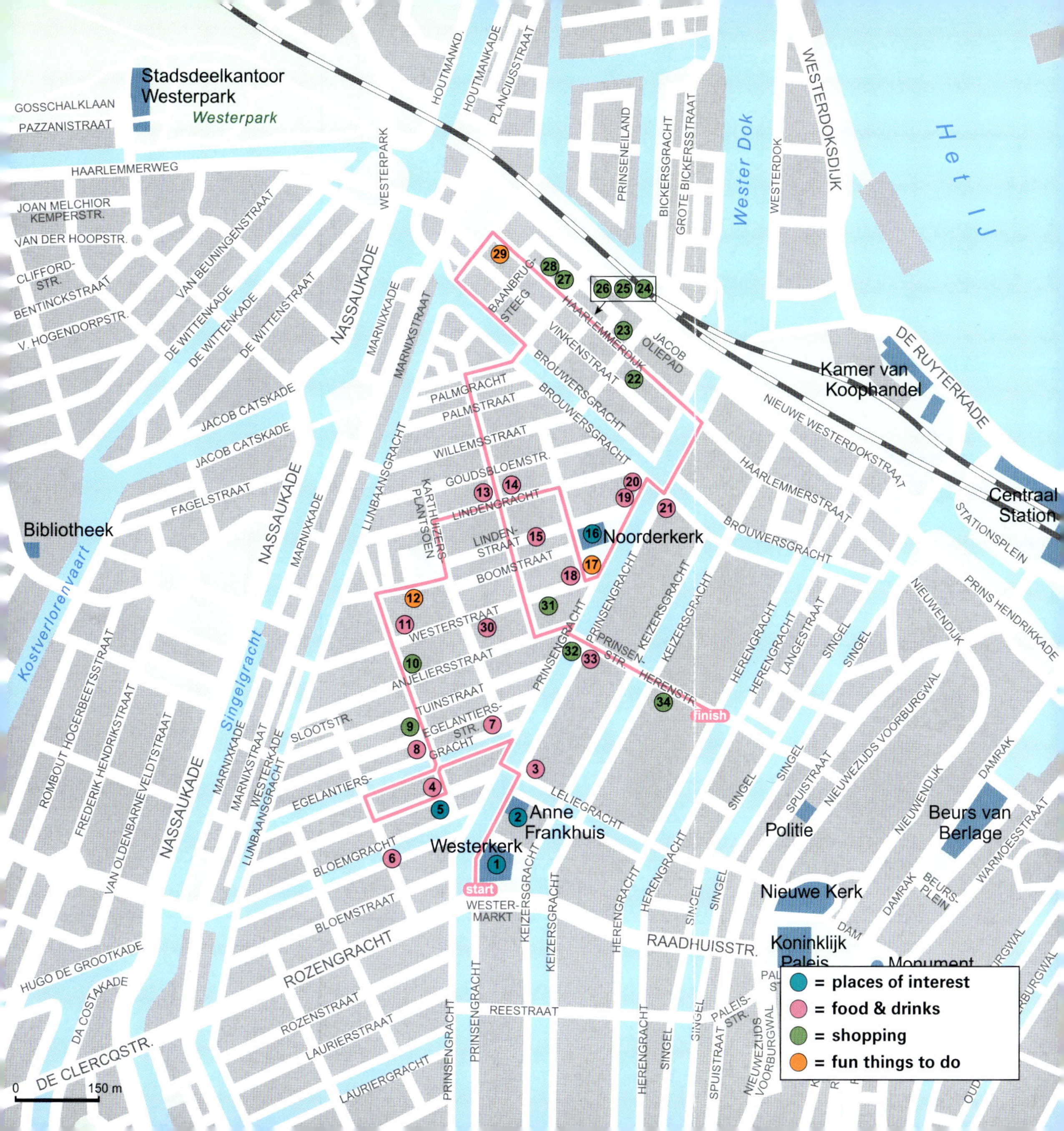
Stadsdeelkantoor Westerpark
Westerpark
GOSSCHALKLAAN
PAZZANISTRAAT
HAARLEMMERWEG
JOAN MELCHIOR KEMPERSTR.
VAN DER HOOPSTR.
CLIFFORD-STR.
BENTINCKSTRAAT
V. HOGENDORPSTR.
VAN BEUNINGENSTRAAT
DE WITTENKADE
DE WITTENSTRAAT
NASSAUKADE
MARNIXKADE
MARNIXSTRAAT
WESTERPARK
HOUTMANKD.
HOUTMANKADE
PLANCIUSSTRAAT
PRINSENEILAND
BICKERSGRACHT
GROTE BICKERSSTRAAT
Wester Dok
WESTERDOK
WESTERDOKSDIJK
Het IJ
DE RUYTERKADE
Kamer van Koophandel
NIEUWE WESTERDOKSTRAAT
HAARLEMMERSTRAAT
Centraal Station
STATIONSPLEIN
PRINS HENDRIKKADE
JACOB CATSKADE
FAGELSTRAAT
Bibliotheek
Kostverlorenvaart
Singelgracht
LIJNBAANSGRACHT
KARTHUIZERS PLANTSOEN
PALMGRACHT
PALMSTRAAT
WILLEMSSTRAAT
GOUDSBLOEMSTR.
LINDENGRACHT
LINDEN-STRAAT
BOOMSTRAAT
WESTERSTRAAT
ANJELIERSSTRAAT
TUINSTRAAT
SLOOTSTR.
EGELANTIERS-STR.
EGELANTIERS-GRACHT
BLOEMGRACHT
BLOEMSTRAAT
ROZENGRACHT
ROZENSTRAAT
LAURIERSTRAAT
LAURIERGRACHT
DE CLERCQSTR.
HUGO DE GROOTKADE
DA COSTAKADE
ROMBOUT HOGERBEETSSTRAAT
FREDERIK HENDRIKSTRAAT
VAN OLDENBARNEVELDTSTRAAT
WESTERKADE
BAANBRUG. STEEG
HAARLEMMERDIJK
VINKENSTRAAT
BROUWERSGRACHT
JACOB OLIEPAD
Noorderkerk
PRINSENGRACHT
KEIZERSGRACHT
HERENGRACHT
PRINSEN-STR.
HERENSTR.
finish
start
LELIEGRACHT
Anne Frankhuis
Westerkerk
WESTER-MARKT
RAADHUISSTR.
REESTRAAT
SINGEL
LANGESTRAAT
SPUISTRAAT
NIEUWEZIJDS VOORBURGWAL
NIEUWENDIJK
DAMRAK
WARMOESSTRAAT
Politie
Beurs van Berlage
Nieuwe Kerk
Koninklijk Paleis
BEURS-PLEIN
DAM
PALEIS-STR.
Monument
0 150 m
1 2 3 4 5 6 7 8 9 10 11 12 13 14 15 16 17 18 19 20 21 22 23 24 25 26 27 28 29 30 31 32 33 34
= places of interest
= food & drinks
= shopping
= fun things to do

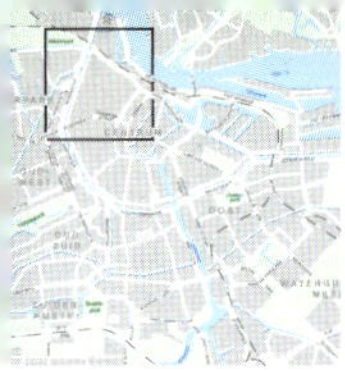

1 Westerkerk
2 Anne Frank Huis
3 Spanjer & Van Twist
4 De Reiger
5 Theo Thijssen Museum
6 Mantoe
7 Café 't Smalle
8 Japanese Pancake World
9 De Kleedkamer
10 Moriaan
11 Cinema Paradiso
12 Karthuizerhofje
13 Kat in de Wijngaert
14 Duende
15 Eetcafé Koevoet
16 Noorderkerk
17 Noordermarkt
18 Winkel 43
19 Proust
20 Papeneiland
21 Café Tabac
22 Restored
23 Papabubble
24 Cellarrich
25 The Silver Screen
26 Vivian Hann
27 Ramona
28 Teuntje
29 The Movies
30 Café Nol
31 Anno
32 Margriet Nannings
33 Letting
34 Outras Coisas

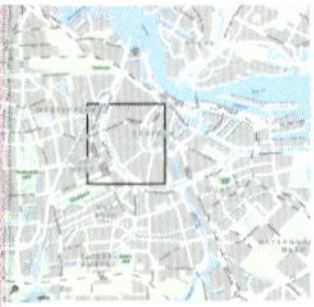

Negen Straatjes

Shopping, design, eclectic and food

'Oh the enchanting Negen Straatjes...' that sounds much nicer than 'Zeven Straatjes plus twee stegen' (Nine streets and Two Alleys) which is what they are in reality. The Reestraat, Hartenstraat,Gasthuis Molensteeg, Berenstraat, Wolvenstraat, Oude Spiegelstraat, Runstraat, Huidenstraat and Wijde Heisteeg make up a delightful area with a mix of coolness, tradition and informality to it. This is the place to be for every shopaholic. Shopping here is incredibly relaxed, compared to the desperate crush in the Kalverstraat. Small boutiques for clothes and shoes (second-hand and new), bijou shops for trendy home accessories and delicatessen, jewellers and hair salons are all jumbled together. New hot spots are opening all the time. Even if you're not that keen on shopping, it's still a great neighbourhood to wander around. Just stroll through streets and admire all the lovely canals and historic buildings.

3

Shopping in the Negen Straatjes is very more-ish. That's why we've also sneaked in the Leidsestraat, a well known Amsterdam shopping street where shopaholics can indulge themselves. For example, there's Metz and Co., Raak and Daryl van Wouw, right on the Prinsengracht. And if you feel like a bit of culture, you don't have to travel far. Just outside the Negen Straatjes on the Spui you'll find the bookstores Atheneum, the American Bookstore and Waterstone's (more towards the Kalverstraat) plus the book market every Friday. Don't forget the Begijnhof, the most famous courtyard (hofje) in Amsterdam, and the Old Masters gallery in the Amsterdam Historical Museum.

6 things not to be missed!

Metz & Co

Admire the view from this deluxe department store.

Pancakes!

Very special pancakes.

Kitsch Kitchen

You'll have fun with their colourful products.

Lady Day

You might just find that vintage treasure.

Brilmuseum

Try on frames both antique and new.

De Kaaskamer

Buy your smelly cheeses!

- **Places of interest**
- **Shopping**
- **Food & drinks**
- **Fun things to do**

Places of interest

(1) Sorry Bijenkorf, but **Metz & Co** is the poshest department store in Amsterdam, especially if you're looking for expensive furniture and designer clothes. The high point is literally the café-restaurant on the top floor. Designed by Gerrit Rietveld, it has a wonderful view over the city.
leidsestraat 34-36, telephone (0031) 020 520 70 20, www.metzenco.nl, open mon 11.00-18.00, tues-sat 9.30-18.00, sunday 12.00-17.00, price € 15, trams 1, 2, 5 keizersgracht

(2) Do wander down the **Reguliersdwarsstraat**. This famous street is the hub of gay Amsterdam. Especially during the Amsterdam Gay Pride Festival, gays (as well as lots of heteros) gather to party at the various stands and stages. There is also a huge selection of different types of restaurants.
trams 1, 2, 5 koningsplein

(17) The Jordanese 'levenslied' (*chanson*-like song) existed long before André Hazes. You'll find the icons of yesteryear on the **Johnny Jordaanplein**, which is actually part of the Elandsgracht. Feel that real Amsterdam nostalgia, watched over by the statues of Johnny himself, Tante Leen, Manke Nelis and Johnny Meyer.
elandsgracht, trams 7, 10 elandsgracht

Food & drinks

(5) Whether or not the **Vlaams Friteshuis** is the best chip shop in the city is debatable. Looking at the queues for its freshly cut and fried Flemish chips however, many Amsterdammers are clearly decided, and have been for years. With mayonnaise of course, but you could also try their Belgian sauces like American, Andalousian, Tartare or lemon mayo.
voetboogstraat 33, telephone (0031) 020 624 60 75, open daily 11.00-18.00, price € 2.30, trams 1, 2, 4, 5, 9, 14, 16, 24, 25 spui

(7) For a delicious salad or generously filled sandwich in an unpretentious lunchroom you can't beat **Lef**. They also serve toasted sandwiches and smoothies. This lunchroom might be small but the portions are huge.
wijde heisteeg 1, telephone (0031) 020 620 57 68, www.lef-amsterdam.nl, open mon-fri 8.00-17.00, sat-sunday 10.00-18.00, price € 9, trams 1, 2, 4, 5, 9, 14, 16, 24, 25 spui

(9) **Goodies** is the perfect place for a quick, reasonably priced pasta or salad. You can also have lunch here after 12am. It has a delightful interior with white-painted tables and benches. There's a small terrace in the summertime.
huidenstraat 9, telephone (0031) 020 625 61 22, www.goforthegoodies.nl, kitchen open mon-wed & Sunday 12.00-22.00, thurs-sat 12.00-22.30, price € 22, trams 1, 2, 4, 5, 9, 14, 16, 24, 25 spui

(15) Order some modest Italian nibbles and a drink and you're all set for a fantastic evening at **Festina Lente**. Inside you can relax in large armchairs or play games, or you can enjoy a sultry summer evening on a bench along the canal.
looiersgracht 40b, telephone (0031) 020 638 14 12, www.cafefestinalente.nl, open mon & sunday 12.00-1.00, tues-thurs 10.30-1.00, fri-sat 10.30-3.00, price € 19, trams 7, 10 elandsgracht

GOODIES ⑨

(16) It must be said, Thai restaurants are usually not terribly atmospheric. You come for the food and then leave. **Rakang Restaurant** is something else altogether. Both food and design are first class. Pleasant lighting, pristine white tablecloths, Versace plates. You'll have a wonderful evening out at Rakang, so be sure to wear your Sunday best.
elandsgracht 29-31, telephone (0031) 020 620 95 51, www.rakang.nl, price € 45, open daily 18.00-22.30, trams 7, 10 marnixstraat

(18) **Pancakes!** is filled with memories of youth as well as new discoveries. Here, the global pancake is celebrated. It's a little pancake heaven, and not just loved by kids. Of course you can order the familiar recipe with bacon, but for the more adventurous eaters they will add banana and a red chili. The setting is old-style Dutch, but you'll also find blinis, crêpes, roti and tortillas on the menu.
berenstraat 38, telephone (0031) 020 528 97 97, www.pancakesamsterdam.nl, open daily 10.00-19.00, price € 12, trams 1, 2, 4, 5, 9, 14, 16, 24, 25 spui

(19) **Nielsen** is a popular breakfast and lunch café. In the mornings, you can enjoy a delicious breakfast with a fresh smoothie, bagel or an omelette. And for lunch, a club sandwich or a salad is a good choice. Make sure you're not in a hurry though, as the service is none too speedy.
berenstraat 19, telephone (0031) 020 330 60 06, open tues-fri 8.00-16.00, sat 8.00-18.00, sunday 9.00-17.00, price € 14, trams 1, 2, 4, 5, 9, 14, 16, 24, 25 spui

(22) **Brix** is a stylish restaurant with dark mirrors and brick walls. The menu offers little bites from all over the world. They have jam sessions every Monday and Sunday evening.
wolvenstraat 16, telephone (0031) 020 639 03 51, www.cafebrix.nl, open mon-thurs 17.00-1.00, fir & sat 17.00-3.00, sunday 17.00-1.00, price € 22, trams 1, 2, 4, 5, 9, 14, 16, 24, 25 spui

(28) It might be a little unusual but it's well worth a visit. **Schuim** is definitely one of the city's better cafés and meeting places. Schuim is a teensy bit 'arty', as artists can exhibit their work. They provide simple meals, and exceptionally good drinks. Weekends are for dancing and flirting!
spuistraat 189, telephone (0031) 020 638 93 57, open sunday-thurs 11.00-1.00, fri-sat 11.00-3.00, price € 17, trams 1, 2, 4, 9, 13, 14, 16, 17, 24, 25 dam

(32) **Van Harte** is a popular restaurant where you can eat and drink in a cheerful atmosphere, both in the afternoons and evenings. The bar is in the centre of the restaurant, and the wallpaper will give you an instant lift.
hartenstraat 24, telephone (0031) 020 625 85 00, www.vanharte.com, open mon 10.00-17.30, tues-sat 10.00-0.00, sunday 11.00-19.00, price € 34, trams 1, 2, 4, 9, 13, 16, 14, 17, 24, 25 dam

Shopping

(3) You can spend hours there. **Selexyz Scheltema** is the largest book store in Amsterdam, and has been for years. Now and then, authors come by for signings and there's a coffee-and-bagel bar inside. There are five floors, with 125,000 titles.
koningsplein 20, telephone (0031) 020 523 14 11, www.selexyz.nl, open mon-wed & fri-sat 10.00-18.00, thurs 10.00-21.00, sunday 12.00-18.00, trams 1, 2, 5 koningsplein

(8) Onitsuka what? **Onitsuka Tiger** is the pilot store for Asics sneakers, but only for classic models (from 1949 to 1985). The brand was originally created to promote self confidence in Japanese youth. They have the very latest unique sneakers and even jeans from this exciting label.
herengracht 356, hoek huidenstraat, telephone (0031) 020 528 61 83, www.onitsukatiger.nl, open mon 13.00-18.00,tues-sat 10.00-18.00, trams 1, 2, 4, 5, 9, 14, 16, 24, 25 spui

(10) Design your very own jewellery. At **Beadies** the baskets overflow with wonderful beads, pendants and other sparkly things. Not too keen on DIY? Don't panic, they also have ready-made earrings, bracelets and necklaces.
huidenstraat 6, telephone (0031) 020 428 51 61, www.beadies.com, open mon 13.00-18.00, tues-wed &fri-sat 10.30-18.00, thurs 10.30-21.00, trams 1, 2, 4, 5, 9, 14, 16, 24, 25 spui

(11) You can buy clothing from Dries van Noten, Ann Demeulemeester, Dirk Bikkembergs and other (Belgian) top designers at **Van Ravenstein**. You simply must go down to the bargain basement where you might just score a find amongst the previous collections.
keizersgracht 359, telephone (0031) 020 639 00 67, www.van-ravenstein.nl, open mon 13.00-18.00, tues-wed & fri 11.00-18.00, thurs 11.00-19.00, sat 10.30-17.30, trams 1, 2, 4, 5, 9, 14, 16, 24, 25 spui

PARISIENNE 21

(12) Although it's not all they have to offer, one famous designer sets the tone at **Local Service's** two corner shops: Paul Smith. The smart suits, the unmistakable stripes and the fabulous accessories are well worth the visit. This one's especially for the men.
keizersgracht 400hs & 402, telephone (0031) 020 626 68 40, open mon-sun 10.00-18.00, trams 1, 2, 4, 5, 9, 14, 16, 24, 25 spui

(13) You can buy cheeses drenched in calvados or decorated with vine leaves and other wonderful creations at **De Kaaskamer**. Cheese freaks know that this aromatic shop is the ultimate place to find a mind-boggling selection of Dutch cheeses, as well as more unusual ones. Nuts and mouth-watering sausages complete the perfect picnic hamper.
runstraat 7, telephone (0031) 020 623 34 83, www.kaaskamer.nl, open mon 12.00-18.00, tues-fri 9.00-18.00, sat 9.00-17.00, sunday 12.00-17.00, trams 1, 2, 4, 5, 9, 14, 16, 24, 25 spui

(14) **Shirts and cappuccino** sells those perfect-fit Italian shirts in the latest fashions from Milan, as well as sweaters, ties, trousers and shoes. Actually, everything except suits. The collection changes regularly and the shirts are hand-made. You can have a delicious cappuccino while you're trying everything on.
runstraat 26, telephone (0031) 020 428 00 93, www.shirtsandcappuccino.nl, open mon 13.00-19.00, tues-wed & fri 11.00-19.00, thurs 11.00-21.00, sat 11.00-18.00, sunday 13.00-17.00, trams 1, 2, 4, 5, 9, 14, 16, 24, 25 spui

(20) **Stout** has lingerie and other frisky stuff for those long, cold winter evenings and sultry summer nights. Stout's tasteful range for both men and women is sure to raise more than just a smile.
berenstraat 9, telephone (0031) 020 620 16 76, www.stoutinternational.com, open mon-fri 12.00-19.00, sat 11.00-18.00, sunday 13.00-17.00, trams 1, 2, 4, 5, 9, 14, 16, 24, 25 spui

(21) **Parisienne** is a wonderfully romantic store selling jewellery from Paris. You'll also find some frivolous handbags and scarves with delicate embroidery, sequins and beads. No doubt you'll buy something lovely.
berenstraat 4, telephone (0031) 020 428 08 34, open tues-fri 10.00-18.00, sat 10.00-17.00, sunday 12.00-17.00, trams 1, 2, 4, 5, 9, 14, 16, 24, 25 spui

MARGARETH MACKENZIE (26)

(23) This isn't a shop; it's a self-confessed concept fashion store. Actually, **Spoiled/Denimbar** is the coolest clothing store with the hippest designer wear. They will even style your hair. Especially wonderful is the Denim Bar where the team will help you find the perfect jeans. Some brands: Nudie jeans, Barong Barong, Stella Nova and Tiger of Sweden.
wolvenstraat 19, telephone (0031) 020 626 38 18, www.spoiled.nl, open mon 12.00-18.00, tues-wed & fri-sat 10.00-18.00, thurs 10.00-19.00, sunday 12.00-18.00, trams 1, 2, 4, 5, 9, 14, 16, 24, 25 spui

(24) More and more people are wearing **Le Coq Sportif** shoes. This French brand has made a real trend revival over the last few years, and in this flagship store you will find the latest complete collection of les sneakers, les T-shirts and other sporty and funky clothes, all with the famous cockerel logo of course.
wolvenstraat 14, telephone (0031) 020 320 40 98, www.lecoqsportif.nl, open mon 13.00-18.00, tues-wed & fri-sat 10.00-18.00, thurs 10.00-21.00, sunday 12.00-18.00, trams 1, 2, 4, 5, 9, 14, 16, 24, 25 spui

(25) If you're looking for vintage clothes from the 40s and 50s, then **Laura Dols** is a must. Rummage through the flowery dresses, ruffled blouses and crocheted tablecloths. Pure nostalgia! At the back, you'll find the 'Verkleedkomeet': a veritable treasure chest full of dressing-up clothes for the kids.
wolvenstraat 6-7, telephone (0031) 020 624 90 66, www.lauradols.nl, open mon & sunday 13.00-18.00, tues-wed & sat 11.00-18.00, thurs & fri 11.00-19.00, trams 1, 2, 4, 5, 9, 14, 16, 24, 25 spui

(26) Do you long for those wonderful markets in Asia? At **Margareth Mackenzie**, you'll find everything that you couldn't fit in your suitcase! Lamps, little tables, pouffes, everything for an ethno-chic interior. For more portable Asiatic riches such as purses, jewellery and scarves, visit the Trunk in the Rosmarijnsteeg at number 12.
oude spiegelstraat 4hs, telephone (0031 020 320 88 66, open mon-thurs 11.00-18.30, sat 11.00-18.00, sunday 12.00-17.00, trams 1, 2, 4, 5, 9, 14, 16, 24, 25 spui

(27) If you want a Finnish shopping experience then go along to **Kauppa** (shop). You'll find a mix of colourful, more restrained and modern fashion, accessories and furniture made in Finland. Think brands like Marimekko, Aarikka and Chao & Eero. Bet you don't leave the shop empty-handed!
oude spiegelstraat 6a, telephone (0031) 020 622 48 48, www.kauppa.nl, open mon 12.00-18.00, tues-sat 11.00-18.00, sunday closed, trams 1, 2, 4, 5, 9, 14, 16, 24, 25

(30) Fashion freaks buy their shoes from **Antonia by Yvette**. Labels include Roberto Botticelli, Roberto Cavalli, Sonia Rykiel, Kop and Staart, Moma, Freelance and Kickers, for both men and women. They also have a small collection of bags.
gasthuismolensteeg 18, telephone (0031) 020 320 94 43, www.antoniabyyvette.nl, open mon 12.00-18.00, tues-sat 10.00-18.00, sunday 13.00-17.00, trams 1, 2, 4, 5, 9, 13, 14, 16, 17, 24, 25 dam

(31) **Lady Day** buys original vintage clothing from all over the world to resell in their shop. Here's where you'll find spotless (leather) jackets, white and coloured shirts, suits, trousers and cocktail- and ball gowns from the 20s to the 80s. They also have a selection of shoes, pumps and accessories.
hartenstraat 9, telephone (0031) 020 623 58 20, open mon-sat 11.00-18.00, sunday 13.00-18.00, trams 1, 2, 4, 5, 13, 14, 16, 17, 24, 25 dam

(33) **Paul Frank**'s creations are all over the world. Everyone knows his T-shirts, bags and sweaters with the famous logo of the ape, who is commonly known as Julius. Fortunately, he now has some little friends, like Clancy the giraffe and Sheree the cat.
hartenstraat 23, telephone (0031) 020 423 25 80, www.paulfrank.com, open mon 12.00-18.00, tues-wed &fri-sat 10.00-18.00, thurs 10.00-21.00, sunday 12.00-18.00, trams 1, 2, 4, 5, 9, 13, 14, 16, 17, 24, 25 dam

(34) It all started at a market stall, selling colourful plastic tablecloths from Mexico. Since then, **Kitsch Kitchen** has blossomed into a cheery *supermercado*. The stunning poppy-red wall, the large plastic shopping trolleys and the countless original gifts made in Mexico and other parts of the world make this store a real shopper's paradise.
rozengracht 8-12, telephone (0031) 020 428 49 69, www.kitschkitchen.nl, open mon-sat 10.00-18.00,sunday 12.00-17.00, trams 13, 14, 17 westermarkt

(35) Lovers of designer furniture can shop to their heart's content in the Kasstoorgroep's three branches on the Rozengracht: **Wonen 2000, Wonen 2000 Bed&Bad** and **de Kasstoor**. They sell top brands including Gispen, Kartel, Linteloo and Edra.
rozengracht 202-210, telephone (0031) 020 521 81 12, www.dekasstoor.nl, open tues-sat 10.00-18.00, trams 3, 14, 17 rozengracht

(36) Shopping in **SPRMRKT** is an absolute delight for anyone who loves collectors' items from the 60s, 70s and 80s. Furniture, bikinis, bathing suits, shirts, ties, scarves and music are laid out over no less than 450 square metres. They also have artwork, occasionally a car and even their own clothing line.
rozengracht 191-193, telephone (0031) 020 330 56 01, www.sprmrkt.nl, open mon & sunday 12.00-18.00, tues-sat 10.00-18.00, thurs 10.00-20.00, trams 3, 14, 17 rozengracht

Fun things to do

(4) You will be surrounded by colours and scents on the **Bloemenmarkt** (Flower market) next to the Singel. The flowers and plants are displayed on permanently moored barges, harking back to the time when the goods were still transported to market by water from the gardens around the city.
singelgracht (between the koningsplein and the muntplein), open mon-sat 9.00-17.30, sunday 11.00-17.30, free, tram 1, 2, 5 koningsplein

(6) Every Friday, there is a **book market** on the Spui. It's fun to rummage around the second-hand and antique books and prints. On Sundays, the Spui is transformed into an art market, where artists can exhibit their paintings and sculptures.
spui, open fri 9.00-18.00, sunday 9.00-17.00, free, trams 1, 2, 4, 5, 9, 14, 16, 24, 25 spui

(29) You can buy all the latest (designer) frames downstairs in the shop. If you want a glimpse back into yesteryear however, the little **Brilmuseum** (spectacle museum) upstairs awaits you: a Valhalla for old frames, like lorgnettes, winged frames, and the Buddy Holly's design. It's fun even if you're not a museum fan.
gasthuismolensteeg 7, telephone 020 421 24 14, www.brilmuseumamsterdam.nl, free , open wed-fri 11.30-17.30, sat 11.30-17.00, trams 1, 2, 4, 5, 9, 13, 14, 16, 17 24, 25 dam

LUNETTES
POUR C
EN AUTOM
Lunette à coqu
bles, grand ma
doublé, avec
et coulant de
Indiquer le tou
en passant su

Negen Straatjes

WALK 3

From the Leidseplein, walk down the Leidsestraat past all the shops and luxurious department store 1 to the Koningsplein to visit the 'pink' street 2 or the book lover's paradise 3. You will see all the flower stalls on the right of the square 4. To carry on shopping, walk from the Koningsplein to the Heiligeweg. Turn left into the Voetboogstraat 5 for the best chips ever, then carry on to the Spui. Don't go into the busy Kalverstraat, because you are now on the square with all the super book shops and book markets 6. From the Spui, turn right into Heisteeg past the famous café Hoppe de Wijde. This is the start of the Negen Straatjes with their extra special boutiques, galleries, lunchrooms and restaurants. Stop for a lovely lunch at Lef's in the Wijde Heisteeg. 7. Walk on to the Huidenstraat for shopping or refreshments 8 9 10 11. Follow the walk via the Runstraat for even more shops 12 13 14. For a touch of Old Amsterdam, cross over the Prinsengracht to the Looiersgracht, where you can drop in at Festina Lente 15. Just before the end, turn right towards the Elandsgracht. Here you'll find a mix of speciality stores, shops for day to day shopping and restaurants, like the Rakang Restaurant 16, one of the best Thai eateries in Amsterdam. Follow the Elandsgracht northwards and you will hit the Johnny Jordaanplein 17 where you will find the statues of four musical idols of the Amsterdam 'levenslied' (*chanson*-like songs): Johnny Jordaan, Tante Leen, Manke Nelis and Johnny Meijer. Actually you've now strayed into the Jordaan, so back up a little. Stop off for very special pancakes then carry on shopping in the Berenstraat 18 19 20 21 and the Wolvenstraat 22 23 24 25. Carry on via the Oude Spiegelstraat for Margareth Mackenzie 26 and Kauppa 27 then turn left into the Spuistraat. Walk to the end for a nice drink 28. You can now turn left into the Paleisstraat. If you want to do more shopping, go into the Gasthuismolensteeg 29 30 and Hartenstraat 31 32 33. Still not satisfied? Cross the bridge right via de Prinsengracht then take the third street on the left into the Rozengracht, where you'll find mostly furniture stores 34 35 36.

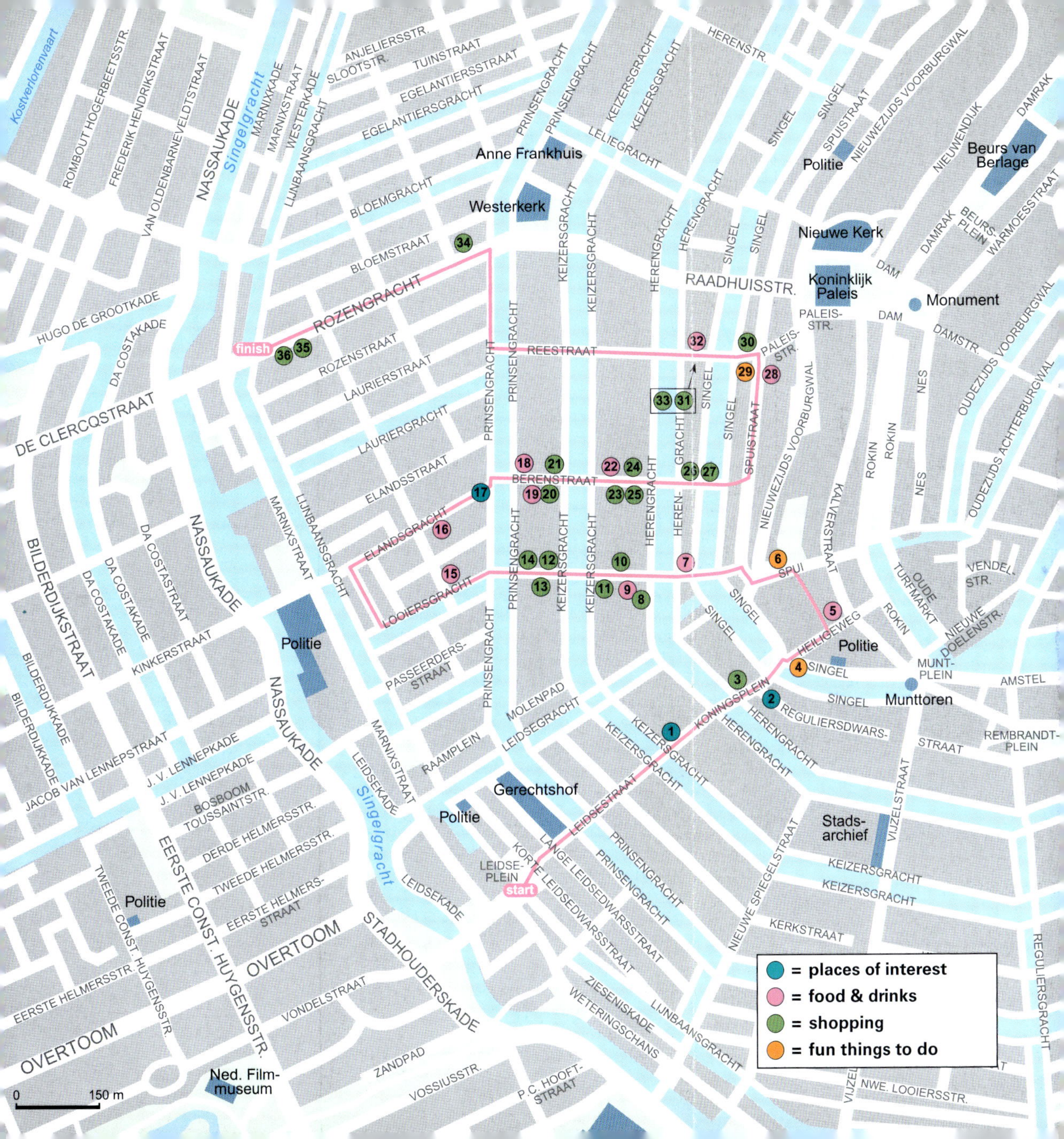

Kostverlorenvaart
Singelgracht
ROMBOUT HOGERBEETSSTR.
FREDERIK HENDRIKSTRAAT
VAN OLDENBARNEVELDTSTRAAT
NASSAUKADE
MARNIXKADE
MARNIXSTRAAT
WESTERKADE
LIJNBAANSGRACHT
ANJELIERSSTR.
SLOOTSTR.
TUINSTRAAT
EGELANTIERSSTRAAT
EGELANTIERSGRACHT
PRINSENGRACHT
KEIZERSGRACHT
HERENSTR.
LELIEGRACHT
SINGEL
SPUISTRAAT
NIEUWEZIJDS VOORBURGWAL
NIEUWENDIJK
DAMRAK
Beurs van Berlage
Politie
Anne Frankhuis
Westerkerk
BLOEMGRACHT
BLOEMSTRAAT
Nieuwe Kerk
Koninklijk Paleis
RAADHUISSTR.
HERENGRACHT
BEURSPLEIN
WARMOESSTRAAT
DAM
Monument
PALEISSTR.
DAMSTR.
OUDEZIJDS VOORBURGWAL
HUGO DE GROOTKADE
DA COSTAKADE
ROZENGRACHT
finish
ROZENSTRAAT
LAURIERSTRAAT
REESTRAAT
LAURIERGRACHT
DE CLERCQSTRAAT
NES
ROKIN
OUDEZIJDS ACHTERBURGWAL
ELANDSSTRAAT
BERENSTRAAT
ELANDSGRACHT
KALVERSTRAAT
BILDERDIJKSTRAAT
DA COSTASTRAAT
SPUI
VENDELSTR.
TURFMARKT
OUDE
LOOIERSGRACHT
HEILIGEWEG
NIEUWE DOELENSTR.
Politie
KINKERSTRAAT
PASSEERDERSSTRAAT
MUNTPLEIN
AMSTEL
BILDERDIJKKADE
KONINGSPLEIN
Munttoren
MOLENPAD
LEIDSEGRACHT
REGULIERSDWARSSTRAAT
REMBRANDTPLEIN
JACOB VAN LENNEPSTRAAT
J. V. LENNEPKADE
RAAMPLEIN
LEIDSEKADE
Gerechtshof
BOSBOOM TOUSSAINTSTR.
Politie
LEIDSESTRAAT
Stadsarchief
VIJZELSTRAAT
DERDE HELMERSSTR.
TWEEDE HELMERSSTR.
EERSTE HELMERSSTRAAT
LEIDSEPLEIN
start
KORTE LEIDSEDWARSSTRAAT
LANGE LEIDSEDWARSSTRAAT
NIEUWE SPIEGELSTRAAT
TWEEDE CONST. HUYGENSSTR.
EERSTE CONST. HUYGENSSTR.
OVERTOOM
STADHOUDERSKADE
KERKSTRAAT
REGULIERSGRACHT
EERSTE HELMERSSTR.
VONDELSTRAAT
ZIESENISKADE
WETERINGSCHANS
LIJNBAANSGRACHT
ZANDPAD
Ned. Filmmuseum
VOSSIUSSTR.
P.C. HOOFTSTRAAT
NWE. LOOIERSSTR.
0 150 m
= places of interest
= food & drinks
= shopping
= fun things to do

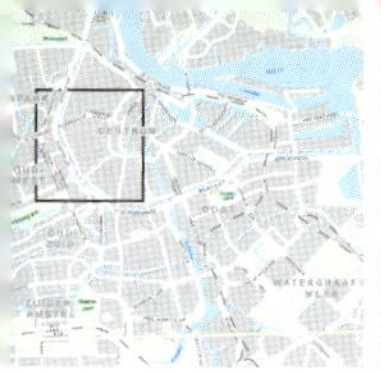

1. Metz & Co
2. Reguliersdwarsstraat
3. Selexyz Scheltema
4. Bloemenmarkt
5. Vlaams Friteshuis
6. Boekenmarkt
7. Lef
8. Onitsuka Tiger
9. Goodies
10. Beadies
11. Van Ravenstein
12. Local Service
13. De Kaaskamer
14. Shirts and cappuccino
15. Festina Lente
16. Rakang Restaurant
17. Johnny Jordaanplein
18. Pancakes!
19. Nielsen
20. Stout
21. Parisienne
22. Brix
23. Spoiled/Denimbar
24. Le Coq Sportif
25. Laura Dols
26. Margareth Mackenzie
27. Kauppa
28. Schuim
29. Brilmuseum
30. Antonia by Yvette
31. Lady Day
32. Van Harte
33. Paul Frank
34. Kitsch Kitchen
35. Wonen 2000 en De Kasstoor
36. SPRMRKT

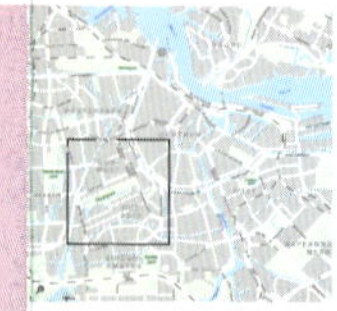

Oud-Zuid & Oud-West

Chic, relaxed, interior, rosé

The swish Museum quarter offers so many cultural places of interest, such as the Rijksmuseum and the Van Gogh Museum. The Stedelijk Museum is also nearby on the corner of Van Baerlestraat and Paulus Potterstraat. Due to a major refurbishment, the museum is temporarily on tour through the city. Until its re-opening in 2010, the Stedelijk will be visiting various sister institutions and appearing in some unexpected places with smaller projects. The exclusive P.C. Hooftstraat also lies in the Museum quarter. This famous street is the shopping mecca for people with overstuffed wallets or a place to show off the latest SUV or sports car. The adjacent district of Oud-West is on the up-and-up. The Helmersbuurt has lovely, quiet streets where you can enjoy a walk and a look at the beautiful houses. The musical duo Acda & De Munnik serenaded the 'Eerste Helmersstraat'.

4

Munnik and the Bosboom Toussaintstraat are two of the most beautiful streets in the city. You can lounge about and have a picnic in the Vondelpark, which is still the most popular park in Amsterdam. Especially in summer, it's one huge open air theatre teeming with roller bladers, joggers, outdoor café enthusiasts, sun worshippers and tourists.

West of the Vondelpark is the Overtoom, where you'll come across a couple of wonderful furniture stores and a real hidden pearl: the Hollandsche Manege (riding school). On the eastern side of the park is Oud-Zuid, one of Amsterdam's wealthiest districts, home to the upper classes (both old and new money). Near to the Cornelis Schuyt- en Jacob Obrechtstraat you'll find a couple of trendy shops as well swish, chic restaurants.

6 things not to be missed!

Rijksmuseum

Admire the works of the Old Masters.

Concertgebouw

Take in a free lunch concert

P.C. Hooftstraat

Good for spending money and watching people.

Hollandsche Manege

Take a look at this riding stable dating from 1882.

Vondelpark

Enjoy a relaxing walk, picnic or sunbathe.

Van Gogh Museum

Take a quiet morning and drink in the art

- **Places of interest**
- **Shopping**
- **Food & drinks**
- **Fun things to do**

Places of interest

(1) The **Rijksmuseum** will be undergoing the biggest renovation in its history until 2013. You can still view The Nachtwacht by Rembrandt van Rijn and works by masters like Johannes Vermeer, Frans Hals and Jan Steen. It's also lovely to stroll around the Museum gardens where you can look at the statues and city gates.
jan luijkenstraat 1, telephone (0031) 020 674 70 00, www.rijksmuseum.nl, open mon-thurs & sat-sunday 9.00-18.00, fri 9.00-20.30, admission adults € 11, children 0-18 years free, trams 2, 5 hobbemastraat, 12 concertgebouw

(4) There isn't another place in the world where you can see as much of Vincent van Gogh's work as at the **Van Gogh Museum**: about two hundred paintings, five hundred drawings, seven hundred letters and his collection of Japanese prints. Follow the process of his development and compare his work with that of other painters.
paulus potterstraat 7, telephone (0031) 020 570 52 00, www.vangoghmuseum.nl, open mon-thurs & sat-sunday 10.00-18.00, fri 10.00-22.00, admission adults € 12.50, children 13-17 years € 2.50, 0-12 years free, trams 2, 3, 5, 12 van baerlestraat, 16, 24 museumplein

(16) The **Vondelkerk** is a magnificent neo-Gothic monument near the Vondelpark. This church was built in 1872 from a design by P.H.J. Cuypers, who was also responsible for the Centraal Station and the Rijksmuseum. At weekends, you can hire the church's large hall, a very special location. But you can also have a party in the **Vondelpark**. Pack a party tent, snacks and drinks and you've got your very own garden party. Don't forget the Open-air Theatre from June to August. You can enjoy dance, plays or music every evening from Wednesday to Saturday all for free.
church: vondelstraat 120d, telephone (0031) 020 520 00 90, www.vondelkerk.nl, trams 1, 3, 12 overtoom/eerste constantijn huygenstraat
park: constantijn huygensstraat (various entrances), www.vondelpark.nl, trams 2, 3, 5, 12 van baerlestraat

(17) You will find the **Hollandsche Manege** (riding school) in a place where you would least expect it. You'll be flabbergasted by this grand building dating from 1882. The lofty indoor ring with its balustrades and glorious stucco work takes you back to the style and grandeur of yesteryear. The riding school is still in use.
vondelstraat 140, telephone (0031) 020 618 09 42, www.dehollandschemanege.nl, opening time vary, free, trams 1, 3, 12 overtoom/eerste constantijn huygensstraat

(19) The **Filmmuseum** contains thousands of international, historic and recent films. In July and August, you can enjoy first class films every Saturday evening in the open air.
vondelpark 3, telephone (0031) 020 589 14 00, www.filmmuseum.nl, open daily 9.00-22.00, admission € 7.80, trams 1, 3, 12 overtoom/eerste constantijn huygensstraat, 2, 5, 7 leidseplein

HOLLANDSCHE MANEGE 17

Food & drinks

(2) The **Cobra Café,** situated on the Museumplein has a broad terrace with a view over the lake and the square. They serve delicious club sandwiches, sushi and salads, and what's more you're right next door the major Amsterdam museums, the Rijks, the Van Gogh and, from 2010, the renovated Stedelijk.
hobbemastraat 18, telephone (0031) 020 470 01 11, www.cobracafe.nl, open daily 10.00-21.00, price € 28, trams 2, 5 hobbemastraat

(6) **Bonjour l'Entrecôte et les Dames**. At this very popular pré-concert restaurant (so come after eight o'clock to avoid being trampled by the classical music lovers) you can only order their tender pre-cut entrecote, served with sauce and chips. The only alternative is sole.
van baerlestraat 47-49, telephone (0031) 020 679 88 88, www.entrecote-et-les-dames.nl, open daily 17.30-23.00, price € 22.50, trams 2, 3, 5, 12 van baerlestraat

(7) **Brasserie Keyzer**, once a finance and business establishment in Oud-Zuid, went through a couple of turbulent years with rather dodgy owners and collapsing lights. But *la grande dame* is slowly regaining her dignity. You will be served genuine (rather pricey) classic dishes: coquilles saint-jacques, tournedos Rossini and fruits de mer. Typically Oud-Zuid.
van baerlestraat 96, telephone (0031) 020 675 18 66, www.brasseriekeyzer.nl, open mon-fri 8.00-1.00, sat-sunday 9.00-1.00, price € 44, trams 2, 3, 5, 12 van baerlestraat

(11) This is a wonderful pavement café on one of the loveliest streets in Amsterdam. **Toussaint** is a haven in the Oud-West. Try their sandwiches with buffalo mozzarella, or smoked ham off the bone with mustard sauce. At 'De Italiaan' on the opposite side you can sample their hot oven pizzas with Italian and Dutch cheeses.
bosboom toussaintstraat 26, telephone (0031) 020 685 07 37, www.bosboom-toussaint.nl, open 10.00-22.00, price € 19, trams 1, 3, 7, 12 eerste constantijn huygensstraat/overtoom

DISH GLOBAL KITCHEN ⑰

⑫ We'll let you in on a little secret. The chef who made Mamouche, the Moroccan restaurant in De Pijp, famous has opened his own restaurant. It's called **Zina**, the food is sublime, and you eat in a truly A Thousand and One Nights-atmosphere. Tajines, fresh fruit and tasty herbs from the Maghrib that you can only dream of.
bosboom toussaintstraat 70 bg, telephone (0031) 020 489 37 07, www.restaurantzina.com, open tues-sunday 18.30-22.00, price € 35, trams 1, 3, 7, 12 eerste constantijn huygensstraat/overtoom

(14) **Lab 111** is in what used to be the pathology/anatomy lab in the grounds of the old Wilhelmina Gasthuis. It's a café-restaurant taking part in the Smart Project Space, a platform for artists. Other people are obviously also very welcome! You'll be treated to a good international cuisine (Johannes van Dam gave it a 9) and there are DJs from Thursday to Saturday evenings.
arie biemondstraat 111, telephone (0031) 020 616 99 94, www.lab111.nl, price € 32, open mon-thurs & sunday 14.00-1.00, fri-sat 14.00-3.00, tram 1 jan pieter heijestraat, tram 7 ten katestraat

(18) You can enjoy a drink, lunch or have dinner In the cosy café-restaurant **Vertigo**. In summer, the huge terrace on the steps of the Film Museum is a popular spot. During winter, you're comfortably inside at wooden tables and benches.
vondelpark 3, telephone (0031) 020 612 30 21, www.vertigo.nl, open daily 10.00-1.00, price € 29, trams 2, 3, 5, 12 van baerlestraat

(20) In **'t Blauwe Theehuis** you'll meet people of all ages on the large outdoor terrace. When it's chilly they switch on electric heaters. There's a DJ in the summer months, and you can dance on Friday, Saturday and Sunday evenings.
vondelpark 5, telephone (0031) 020 662 02 54, www.blauwetheehuis.nl, open sunday 9.00-0.00, fri 9.00-3.00, sat 9.00-2.00, price € 30, trams 2, 3, 5, 12 van baerlestraat

(21) **Dish global kitchen** offers the tastiest sandwiches from far flung parts of the world. Could you fancy a Wooley Wooley from Oceania or a Mozambique Shuffle from Africa? Not the traditional cheese sandwich then. Instead you get exotic, healthy creations, served on organic bread. If the weather's good, order a picnic basket because the Vondelpark is just around the corner. Every Sunday, there's live music at the Dish.
overtoom 255, telephone (0031) 020 616 58 35, www.dishglobalkitchen.nl, open tues-sat 11.00-17.00, sunday 12.00-17.00, price € 4.50, tram 1 overtoom

GENT AAN DE SCHINKEL ㉕

⑭ **LAB 111**

㉕ In the city, but not quite part of it; that's how it feels at **Gent aan de Schinkel**. This is a café-restaurant with a wonderful selection of Trappist beers and a view of the boats sailing into the city via the Schinkel.
theophile de bockstraat 1, telephone (0031) 020 388 28 51, www.gentaandeschinkel.nl, price € 20, open mon-thurs & sunday 11.00-1.00, fri-sat 11.00-2.00, tram 1 overtoomsesluis, tram 2 hoofddorpplein

(26) **Sophia** is top chef Ron Blaauw's brainchild. This lady offers tapas, though really they should be called exquisite appetizers. Imagine oysters with a gratin of lime and wasabi or rilettes with sour dough crostini, or simply enjoy a cocktail with or without alcohol.
sophialaan 55, telephone (0031) 020 305 27 60, www.restaurantsophia.nl, open mon-fri 12.00-1.00, sat-sunday 16.00-1.00, price € 34, tram 2 amstelveenseweg

(29) **Affourtit** is an enjoyable local restaurant with a Mediterranean ambience. The internationally orientated menu offers a large choice and changes every two months. During summer you can enjoy your meal outdoors. If the weather takes a turn for the worse, the heaters on the terrace are turned on, or they lend you an Affourtit fleece blanket.
koninginneweg 209, telephone (0031) 020 679 84 17, www.affourtit.nl, open sat-thurs 17.00-1.00, fri 17.00-2.00, price € 28, tram 2 valeriusplein

(30) If you fancy eating in a nice brasserie-type restaurant, then try the **Palma**. The delicious food, fine wines and comfy atmosphere encourage you to linger over your meal.
johannes verhulststraat 104, telephone (0031) 020 379 59 00, www.restaurant-palma.nl, open mon-sat 12.00-23.00, price € 35, tram 2 jacob obrecht-straat

(32) It's not exactly eye catching, but that doesn't take anything away from the quality: **Sal Gorda** is a tapas bar with Spanish waiters. The menu offers familiar dishes like *patatas bravas*, shrimps in garlic oil and hot chicken. Order a *carajillo* (espresso with liqueur) for afters.
van breestraat 107 hs, telephone (0031) 020 673 08 77, www.salgorda.nl, open mon-thurs 17.30-22.30, fri-sat 17.00-23.00, sunday 17.00-22.30, price € 20, tram 2 valeriusplein

(34) **Café Gruter** has been a popular 'bruine kroeg' (old-style pub) for students and locals for years. On Friday afternoons, this is where lots of people start their weekends. For other days and evenings it's the perfect spot for a drink and an appetizer.
willemsparkweg 75, telephone (0031) 020 679 62 52, open sunday-thurs 12.00-1.00, fri-sat 12.00-2.00, price € 2, tram 2 jacob obrechtstraat

Shopping

(8) The chic **P.C. Hooftstraat** is still synonymous with the famous fashion designer labels such as Louis Vuitton, DKNY, Dolce & Gabbana, Gucci, Armani and Hugo Boss. You'll also come across lots of expensive cars, Dutch celebrities and sometimes you can even hear Russian... Quite a sight.
p.c. hooftstraat, opening times vary per shop, trams 2, 3, 5, 12 van baerlestraat

(9) Health food, pure products: no longer the exclusive province of the back-to-nature brigade. Just try **Marqt**, a wonderful supermarket for your daily, farm-fresh and natural food shopping. By the way, they only accept 'plastic money' here.
overtoom 21, telephone (0031) 020 422 63 11, www.marqt.com, mon-sat 8.00-21.00, sunday12.00-18.00, trams 3, 12 overtoom

(10) **Helden en Boeven**, (Heroes and Villains) what a great name for a great business. Helden en Boeven is a brilliant children's book store, which also organises many a film- and other (birthday)-activity for the smaller customers who are fed up with the Artis Zoo.
bosboom toussaintstraat 27, telephone (0031) 020 427 44 07, www.heldenboeven.nl, open mon 13.00-18.00, tues-fri 10.00-18.00, sat 10.00-17.00, trams 1, 3, 7, 12 eerste constantijn huygensstraat/overtoom

(13) How a small shop can be a giant. **Vleck** sells unusual wines from unkown regions, mostly from small farmers. Bought with love and sold with expertise.
eerste helmersstraat 63 hs, telephone (0031) 020 683 59 80, www.vleck.nl, open mon 14.00-19.00, tues-fri 10.30-19.00, sat 10.00-18.00, trams 1, 3, 7, 12 eerste constantijn huygensstraat/overtoom

(15) Travel-mad Amsterdammers already know this: **Pied à Terre** is the best, largest and nicest travel book store in Amsterdam and far beyond. It has a coffee bar, a huge collection of travel guides, globes, hiking maps and everything for even the most timid traveller.
overtoom 135-137, telephone (0031) 020 627 44 55, www.piedaterre.nl, open mon 13.00-18.00, tues-wed & fri 10.00-18.00, thurs 10.00-21.00, sat 10.00-17.00, trams 1, 3, 7, 12 eerste constantijn huygensstraat/overtoom

23

9

(24) **ARI**

(22) In the **Jan Pieter Heijestraat** you'll find excellent cafés, Indonesian shops, quirky shops and a couple of nice bars. It's not on a par with the Negen Straatjes but tourists don't come here much and as a consequence, prices are lower. Dive down some of the side streets! Jan Pieter Heije was actually a doctor and musician.
jan pieter heijestraat, trams 1, 7, 17 jan pieter heijestraat

(23) For Fifties, Sixties and Seventies design, you must go to **Design Overtoom**. This shop is crammed full of lamps and furniture from famous Italian designers.
overtoom 371, 372, telephone (0031) 020 689 81 50, www.designovertoom.nl, open tues-fri 10.00-18.00, sat 11.00-17.00, tram 1 jan pieter heijestraat

(24) Vintage helmets, chains, jackets, bags, glasses, shoes... Dutch celebrities have already discovered **Ari**, but he doesn't make a big deal of it; his prices are still reasonable. You're also very welcome if you only want to browse and not buy, or have a chat.
overtoom 532, telephone (0031) 06 46 32 51 59, open mon-sat 10.00-17.30, tram 1 overtoomsesluis

(27) No wonder they call it 'the childrens' shop with a difference'. At **Imagine** you'll find unique, hand-made gifts and original toys, games, clothing and furniture for babies and toddlers. All-in-all a happy experience.
amstelveenseweg 131, telephone (0031) 020 670 88 99, www.imagine.biz, open mon 13.00-18.00, tues-fri 10.00-18.00,sat 10.00-17.00, tram 2 zeilstraat

(28) **Casa & Luce** is really worth a visit if you're looking for that perfect gift for yourself or someone else. Besides larger pieces of furniture they have lamps, cushions, jewellery and lots of other accessories. All the latest trends, from Dutch to Italian. Exhausted from shopping? You'll find Casa & Cucina right next door – the owner's cheerful lunch room.
koninginneweg 220 hs, telephone (0031) 020 671 65 04, www.casaeluce.com, open mon 12.00-18.00, tues-wed & fri 10.00-18.00, thurs 10.00-21.00, sat 10.00-17.00, tram 2 zeilstraat

(31) **Menno Kroon** makes the most exquisite creations for every occasion using the most beautiful flowers. Not your average bunch, these are real bouquets.
cornelis schuytstraat 11, telephone (0031) 020 679 19 50, www.mennokroon.nl, open mon-fri 9.00-18.00,sat 9.00-17.30, tram 2 cornelis schuytstraat

(33) It's a bit expensive but you do get something really special.The shoes at **Luuks** are all hand-made from the finest leather. For the fans: Jeffrey West, Paul Smith, N.D.C., Freelance and R. Soles. The latter is Madonna's and Victoria Beckham's favourite brand.
jacob obrechtstraat 12, telephone (0031) 020 670 45 38, www.luuks.nl, open mon 13.00-19.00, tues-fri & sat 11.00-18.00, tram 2 jacob obrechtstraat

Fun things to do

(3) The **Museumplein** is a bit worse for wear, and it's only ten years since the square underwent major renovations. In the coming years, this very special piece of Amsterdam is going to be revamped yet again. The square is now a vast area with trees, gravel paths, benches and a lake. In winter you can have fun skating on the ice rink and during summer, it's packed with museum visitors, footballers and sunbathers with bottles of wine and nibbles.
trams 2, 3, 5, 12 museumplein

(5) Amsterdam's **Concertgebouw** is one of the most-visited (and finest!) classical concert halls in the world and famous for its perfect accoustics. You have to book well in advance for a concert, or you could also try catching a free lunch concert – every Wednesday afternoon from 12.30 to 13.00 (but do come early).
concertgebouwplein 10, telephone (0031) 020 671 83 45, www.concertgebouw.nl, trams 2, 3, 5, 12 museumplein

MUSEUMPLEIN ③

Oud-Zuid & Oud-West

WALK 4

Welcome to the Museumplein. Start at the Rijksmuseum (1). On the square, have a drink at the Cobra Café (2). On the Museumplein (3) there is an ellipse-shaped building that forms part of the Van Gogh Museum (4). Walk towards the Concertgebouw (5) and turn into the Van Baerlestraat for a bite to eat (6) (7). You need to turn into the Paulus Potterstraat for the Van Gogh Museum. Would you rather go shopping? Walk on as far as the P.C. Hooftstraat (8). You'll find an alternative to the farmers' market on the right on the Overtoom (9). Go over the crossing and turn into the Tweede Helmersstraat, then left into the Genestetstraat. You are now in the Bosboom Toussaintstraat, for the children's shops (10) and restaurants (11) (12). Carry on to the Eerste Constantijn Huygensstraat and turn left, towards Overtoom. Via Vleck (13) you can walk to the Tweede Constantijn Huygensstraat. Try the Lab111 for some good food (14), or turn right onto the Overtoom for the best travel book store in the city (15). From the Tweede Constantijn Huygensstraat, walk into the Vondelpark past the Vondelkerk (16) and the Hollandsche Manege (17). A bit further on you will see Vertigo (18) and the Film Museum (19). Or you could turn right to relax on the grass or drink a glass of rosé at 't Blauwe Theehuis (20). Leave the park through one of the the side gates on the right and carry on strolling along the Overtoom for some great lunch cafés and interior and vintage shops (21) (22) (23) (24). At the end of the Overtoom, carry on over the bridge and bear left into the Sloterkade, absolutely *the* place for a beer on the waterfront (25). Cross over the cycle bridge towards the Vondelpark and turn right into the Amstelveense Weg. Pop into Sophia (26) for some trendy tapas and do some shopping for the kids further on (27). Turn left into the Koninginneweg for a most unusual shop (28), and for a nutritious rest, go to the Willemsparkweg (29) and turn right into the Emmastraat. Turn left into the Johannes Verhulststraat (30) and wander past the posh shops on the Cornelis Schuytstraat (31). Now turn right into the Van Breestraat for a small Spanish restaurant (32) then take a left for yet another shopping street: the Jacob Obrechtstraat (33). Finish off your walk at the locals' favourite pub: Café Gruter (34).

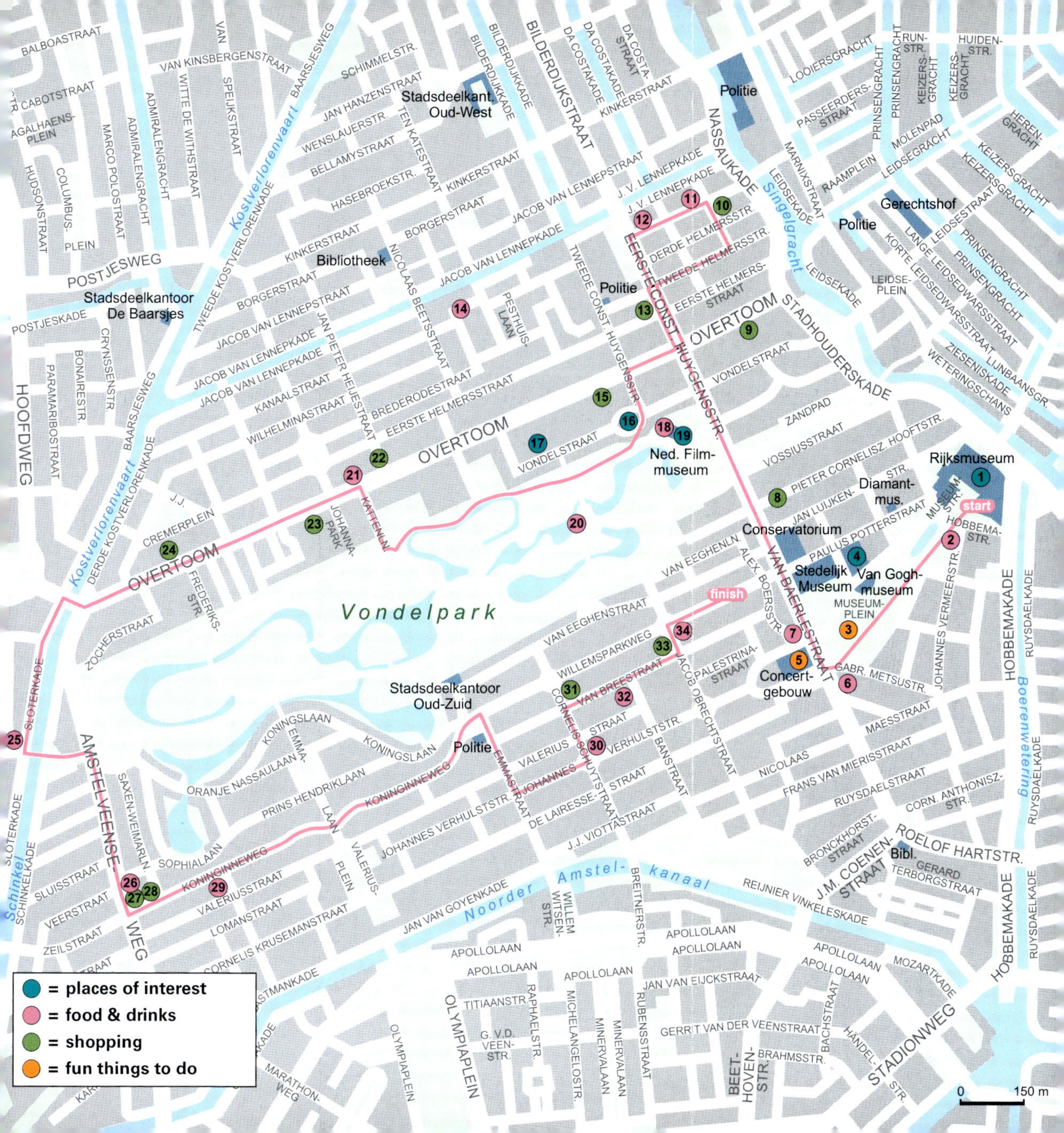

= places of interest
= food & drinks
= shopping
= fun things to do
start
finish
Vondelpark
Rijksmuseum
Diamant-mus.
Conservatorium
Stedelijk Museum
Van Gogh-museum
MUSEUM-PLEIN
Concert-gebouw
Ned. Film-museum
Stadsdeelkant. Oud-West
Stadsdeelkantoor De Baarsjes
Stadsdeelkantoor Oud-Zuid
Bibliotheek
Politie
Gerechtshof
Bibl.
Kostverlorenvaart
Singelgracht
Noorder Amstel-kanaal
Boerenwetering
Schinkel
OVERTOOM
VONDELSTRAAT
STADHOUDERSKADE
EERSTE CONST. HUYGENSSTR.
VAN BAERLESTRAAT
PIETER CORNELISZ. HOOFTSTR.
KONINGINNEWEG
AMSTELVEENSEWEG
HOBBEMAKADE
STADIONWEG
OLYMPIAPLEIN
BILDERDIJKSTRAAT
NASSAUKADE
LEIDSEPLEIN
POSTJESWEG
HOOFDWEG
CORNELIS SCHUYTSTRAAT
JACOB OBRECHTSTRAAT
APOLLOLAAN
0 150 m

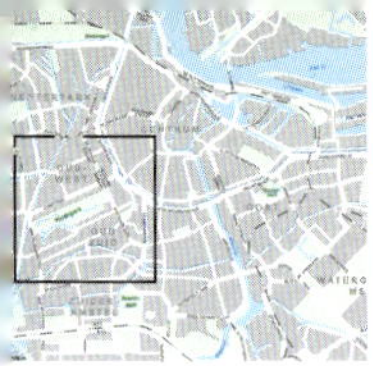

1. Rijksmuseum
2. Cobra Café
3. Museumplein
4. Van Gogh Museum
5. Concertgebouw
6. Entrecôte et les Dames
7. Brasserie Keyzer
8. P.C. Hooftstraat
9. Marqt
10. Helden en Boeven
11. Toussaint
12. Zina
13. Vleck
14. Lab111
15. Pied à Terre
16. Vondelkerk & Vondelpark
17. Hollandsche Manege
18. Vertigo
19. Filmmuseum
20. 't Blauwe Theehuis
21. Dish global kitchen
22. Jan Pieter Heijestraat
23. Design Overtoom
24. Ari
25. Gent aan de Schinkel
26. Sophia
27. Imagine
28. Casa & Luce
29. Affourtit
30. Palma
31. Menno Kroon
32. Sal Gorda
33. Luuks
34. Café Gruter

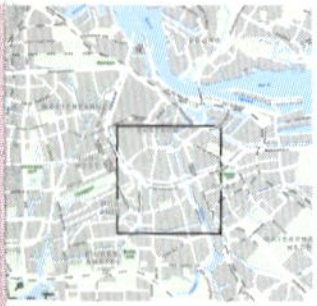

Rembrandtplein, Utrechtsestraat & De Pijp

Etnic, trendy, Hazes

In this part of the city, you'll discover various worlds-within-worlds. The atmosphere of the Rembrandtplein's atmosphere is in sharp contrast to that of the Utrechtsestraat.
In the bars around the square, the motto is clearly 'fun before everything', while the Utrechtsestraat is all about style. It's one of the most beautiful shopping streets in Amsterdam. Many of the people who live in the houses on the canals come here for their Saturday shopping in this lovely street with its very special shops, restaurants and cafés. The museums in this area are less well-known. Alongside the canals you'll find theTassenmuseum (bags), the Kattenkabinet (cats), the Foam (photography) and the Museum van Loon. As well as seeing their unusual collections and exhibitions, you can also sneak a peak behind the facades of the grand houses along the canal. Around Carré and the Magere Brug you can enjoy the peace and admire the stately houses. Don't forget to take a look at the world famous Amstel Hotel, which has hosted such stars as the Rolling Stones and Madonna.

5

Madonna, not to mention members of certain royal families. Their high tea is quite simply superb.

On the other side of the Amstel, the neighbourhood's character gradually changes from stylish and chic to multicultural and trendy. Welcome to De Pijp! This used to be a working-class area, where, among others, André Hazes was born, but now it's the hippest neighbourhood in the city. It's Amsterdam's answer to Le Marais in Paris, or London's Notting Hill. One trendy restaurant after the other is opening its doors between the Surinamese supermarket, the Turkish sewing shops and the Muslim butchers. The renovated 19th century buildings are much in demand by two-income families and entrepreneurs. And that's not really surprising, as the convivial Albert Cuypmarkt and the Sarphatipark are just a stone's throw away. The bustling Pijp is also a magnet for students.

6 things not to be missed!

Tassenmuseum Hendrikje

Admire their collection of around four thousand bags.

Schiller

Have a drink in this lovely art-deco café.

Amstel

Watch the lights from the bridge at night.

Utrechtsestraat

Find unusual clothes, shoes and gadgets.

Albert Cuypmarkt

Mooch around and shop for really good prices.

L'Ozio

Enjoy Italian food and films.

- Places of interest
- Shopping
- Food & drinks
- Fun things to Do

Places of interest

(1) **De Munt** (the Mint) was originally part of the Regulierspoort that itself formed part of the city wall in the Middle Ages. The tower was named in 1672, when it was no longer safe to transport gold and silver to the mints in Dordrecht and Enkhuizen. Amsterdam was granted the temporary right to mint coins in this former guardhouse.
muntplein, trams 4, 9, 16, 24, 25 munt

(8) Photography lovers can browse to their heart's content in **Foam**, Amsterdam's photography museum. You'll come across the work of some big names here including Man Ray and Lee Miller, but it also shows some lesser known talents. It's both a historic and a contemporary museum.
keizersgracht 609, telephone (0031) 020 551 65 00, www.foam.nl, open mon-wed & sat-sunday 10.00-18.00, thurs-fri 10.00-21.00, admission adults € 7.50, children 0-12 years free, trams 16, 24, 25 keizersgracht

(9) **Museum Van Loon** is situated in a canal-side house dating from 1672. Their collection of group portraits is exhibited in amongst 18th century furniture, porcelain and silver. At the back of the house, there are spacious gardens in the French style and an impressive coach house .
keizersgracht 672, telephone (0031) 020 624 52 55, www.museumvanloon.nl, open mon & wed-sunday 11.00-17.00, admission € 6, trams 16, 24, 25 keizersgracht

(15) **The Magere brug (Thin Bridge)** is one of the most beautiful (lift) bridges in Amsterdam, and gets illuminated every evening with thousands of lovely little lights. The Mager ladies, two immensely wealthy sisters who lived on opposite sides of the Amstel, had the bridge built so that it was easier to visit each other.
amstel, tussen de keizersgracht en de prinsengracht (continuation of the kerkstraat), tram 4 prinsengracht

Food & drinks

(3) Since many, many years, **Van Dobben** has been the address for the tastiest sandwiches in Amsterdam, maybe in the whole of the Netherlands. Order a sandwich with rissole and saté sauce, roast beef or liver and beef. The friendly, top-speed service is spiced with typical Amsterdam friendliness and humour.
korte reguliersdwarsstraat 5, telephone (0031) 020 624 42 00, www.vandobben.nl, open mon-thurs 9.30-1.00, fri-sat 9.30-2.00, sunday 11.30-20.00, price € 4.50, trams 4, 9, 14 rembrandtplein

(4) **Café Schiller** is quite different from the other bars around the Rembrandtplein because of its original art-deco design and unique atmosphere. Schiller has style. It's a marvellous place for a drink, or to pop into after a performance at Tuschinski or De Kleine Komedie. Both the appetizers and the food in the restaurant are above average.
rembrandtplein 24-a, telephone (0031) 020 624 98 46, www.cafeschiller.nl, open sunday-thurs 16.00-1.00, fri-sat 16.00-3.00, price € 30, trams 4, 9, 14 rembrandtplein

(13) The café-restaurant **Nel** has the finest terrace in the whole of Amsterdam. Order their fish-dish or the cheese board and sit under the wingnut trees and admire the view over the Prinsengracht. Every Monday, there is a plant- and flower market next to Nel.
amstelveld 12, telephone (0031) 020 626 11 99, www.nelamstelveld.nl, price € 15, open mon-thurs & sunday 10.00-1.00, fri-sat 10.00-3.00, tram 4 prinsengracht

(17) **Amstelhaven** occupies the most beautiful spot, right on the water. Ideal for lunch or a nice drink (and snack). Lots of thirty-somethings come here after work. They crank up the music later in the evenings and there's dancing at the weekend.
mauritskade 1, telephone (0031) 020 665 26 72, www.amstelhaven.nl, open Sunday-wed 11.00-1.00, fri-sat 11.00-3.00, price € 32, trams 7, 10 weesperplein

18

23

(18) Don't expect any culinary highlights at the **Ysbreker**. Having said that, it's a fabulous grand café for a drink. The Ysbreker takes its name from the ship that carved a channel through the frozen Amstel in the 17th Century.
weesperzijde 23, telephone (0031) 020 468 18 08, www.ysbrekercafe.nl, open sunday-thurs 9.00-1.00, fri-sat 9.00-2.00, price € 18, trams 7, 10 weesperplein, 3 amsteldijk

(19) Tiny French-orientated bar in a forgotten street in De Pijp. You can also dine quite royally at the **Klokspijs,** even if you're on a restricted budget. Restaurant guru Johannes van Dam gave this restaurant a 10, and since then it's been chock-a-bloc and rightly so.
hemonystraat 38, telephone (0031) 020 364 25 60, www.klokspijs.nl, open tues-sat 18.00-22.00, price € 20, tram 3 amsteldijk, trams 4, 25 ceintuurbaan

(21) Rotterdammers will recognise the name **Bazar** from the branch in their own city. This Arabic-Turkish concept has also taken the capital by storm. Do visit this fabulous, large *Kasbah* for fresh mint tea, Turkish beer or Arabian grilled dishes. Plenty of food for a modest price.
albert cuypstraat 182, telephone (0031) 020 675 05 44, www.bazaramsterdam.nl, open mon-thurs 11.00-1.00, fri 11.00-2.00, sat 9.00-2.00, sunday 9.00-0.00, price € 18, tram 16, 24 albert cuypstraat

(23) The **Chocolate Bar** is for seeing and being seen in a Sixties/Seventies interior. Join the beautiful people; order a cocktail and a trendy appetiser like dim sum or good old bitterballen (meat croquette) from Van Dobben. The bench outside is the perfect place to sit in summer.
eerste van der helststraat 62a, telephone (0031) 020 675 76 72, www.chocolate-bar.nl, open mon-thurs 10.00-1.00, fri-sat 10.00-3.00, sunday 11.00-1.00, price € 16, trams 16, 24 albert cuypstraat, tram 3 tweede van der helststraat

(25) **Café Krull** has yummy sandwiches, a terrace, plenty of beers on tap and a reading table. It's a haven of peace and as such is much loved by the locals.
sarphatipark 2, telephone (0031) 020 662 02 14, open mon-sat 10.30-18.00, sunday 11.00-18.00, price € 12, trams 16, 24 albert cuypstraat, trams 3, 25 eerste van der helststraat

CHOCOLATE BAR (23)

30

LOVE
het BALKON
ALLE 13 GOED!
ZATERDAG 7 JUNI 2008
A CLASSIC friday
90'S NOW
VIGGO WAAS & BAND
DOKU. ARTS
25

(27) At **Burgermeester,** they make their standard burger from the blonde d'Aquitaine beef, their lamb burger from Texel lamb, on top of which there are the risotto burger, the Spanish burger and the goat's cheese burger to choose from. There's also a branch in the Jordaan and in the Artis Zoo.
albert cuypstraat 48, www.burgermeester.eu, telephone (0031) 020 670 93 39, open daily 12.00-23.00, price € 10, trams 16, 24 albert cuypstraat

(28) Wood ovens are scarce in the city, but they do make the most delicious pizzas, something they know all about at **Da Portare Via**, a tiny pizzeria where you can pick up your pizza to take home, eat it at one of the tables there, or even outside. There's no factory-made sauce here, everything is freshly made.
frans halsstraat 63, no telephone, www.daportarevia.nl, open daily 17.00-22.00, price € 10 (cash only!), trams 16, 24 albert cuypstraat

(29) You can buy the most wonderful cakes ever at **De Taart van m'n Tante**, a place that catches your eye with its cheerful and colourful stuff in the lunchroom. Just looking at the fancy cakes in the window makes your mouth water. Always busy, always fabulous.
ferdinand bolstraat 10, telephone (0031) 020 776 46 00, www.detaart.com, open daily 10.00-18.00, price € 7, trams 16, 24 marie heinekenplein

(30) Italian food, Italian art and Italian films all in one place, and imagine sitting there discussing your choices with the chef and the sommelier. You can even spend hours leafing through the design books from their own library. **L'Ozio** is a modern culture centre with a passion for La Bella Italia.
ferdinand bolstraat 26, telephone (0031) 020 470 81 83, www.ozioamsterdam.com, price € 13, open tues-thurs & sunday 11.00-0.00, fri-sat 11.00-1.00, trams 16, 24 marie heinekenplein

(35) You won't find any fancy creations with macadamia nuts and caramel swirls here. No, it's just lemon, raspberry or pistachio ice cream at **IJscuypje,** but they are all made with fresh ingredients. This means that you'll find real pistachio nuts in the green ice cream. This ice cream has quickly made a name for itself as the best in the city.
eerste van der helststraat 27, telephone (0031) 020 479 55 65, opening times vary per season, price € 3, trams 16, 24 albert cuypstraat, tram 3 tweede van der helststraat

Shopping

(6) Looking for a special piece of jewellery? Then you're bound to find it at **Leonore Sieraden**. The owner, Ilja, travels regularly to Copenhagen to find hand-made jewelerry. Gold and silver set with precious stones and pearls that seem to have come directly from ancient times. Perfect for a special occasion.
utrechtsestraat 53, telephone (0031) 020 624 56 55, open tues-fri 10.00-18.00, sat 10.00-17.00, tram 4 utrechtsestraat

(7) **Studio Bazar** sells everything you could possibly need in the kitchen, from chopping boards to sets of knives, from espresso machines to timers. Anyone who enjoys fancy cooking simply cannot miss this place.
keizersgracht 709, telephone (0031) 020 622 28 58, www.studiobazar.nl, open mon-wed & fri-sat 10.00-18.00, thurs 10.00-21.00, trams 4, 9, 14 rembrandtplein

(10) **Concerto** is a specialist music shop where you can rummage happily for hours. They also have a small second-hand CD department and a desk where you can hand in your old CDs. It's quite simply the best address for first-class music that you can't or don't want to download.
utrechtsestraat 52-60, telephone (0031) 020 623 52 28, www.concerto.nu, open mon-wed & fri-sat 10.00-18.00, thurs 10.00-21.00, sunday 12.00-18.00, tram 4 prinsengracht

(11) The shop windows at **Look Out** have a pulling power that few can resist. For women, there are clothes by Paul Smith, King Louie, Kookaï and Bruuns Bazaar, among others. Look Out for men is on the opposite side of the street.
utrechtsestraat 91-93, telephone (0031) 020 625 50 32, www.lookoutmode.nl, open mon 12.00-18.00, tues-wed & fri 10.00-18.00, thurs 10.00-19.00, sat 10.00-17.00, tram 4 prinsengracht

(12) **Jan** is an unusual shop where you can buy anything and everything. Books, home and interior, bags made by young designers, belts and jewellery. It's an ideal place to find that special gift you're looking for.
utrechtsestraat 74, telephone (0031) 020 626 43 01, open mon 13.00-18.00, tues-fri 11.00-18.30, sat 11.00-18.00, sunday 13.00-18.00, tram 4 prinsengracht

RAAK (33)

24

DUIKELMAN
26

La Grenoui
12

(14) Go inside **A la Carte** and you'll find the world at your feet. This store is jam-packed with street maps, road maps and travel guides for cyclists, walkers, climbers, divers and watersporters. They also have some wonderful travel- and photo books.
utrechtsestraat 110-112, telephone (0031) 020 625 06 79, www.reisboekhandel-alacarte.nl, open mon 13.00-18.00, tues-wed & fri 10.00-18.00, thurs 10.00-21.00, sat 10.00-17.30, sunday 12.00-17.00, tram 4 prinsengracht

(22) Oh how the aroma of spices wafts towards you. At **De Peperbol** you will find hundreds of well known-and not so well known spices from all over the world, from basil to fenugreek seeds and vanilla to cardamom. Everything you need to give your culinary creations that magic touch. You can also order online.
albert cuypstraat 150, telephone (0031) 06 21 50 21 84, www.depeperbol.nl, open mon-sat 8.30-17.30, trams 16, 24 albert cuypstraat

(24) **Tjins** is a global store-literally. Here you can get delicious Surinamese bread rolls with pom, salted meat or cha siu. You could also choose a lunchbox and go off and enjoy it in the nearby Sarphatipark. It's not just a shop for oriental groceries, they also sell lots of lovely things from other parts of the world: English mustard, American barbecue sauce and Mexican spices.
eerste van der helststraat 64, telephone (0031) 020 671 77 08, open mon-sat 10.00-19.30, trams 16, 24 albert cuypstraat, trams 3, 25 tweede van der helststraat

(26) Both culinary amateurs and true catering professionals know that there's really only one place to buy pots, pans, meat thermometers, steak knives, lobster shears, garlic presses -need we go on? You will be able to choose from the biggest and best selection of kitchen utensils at the experts: **Duikelman**. Even if you can't cook.
ferdinand bolstraat 68-68a, telephone (0031) 020 671 22 30, www.duikelman.nl, open tues-fri 9.30-18.00, sat 9.30-17.00, trams 16, 24 albert cuypstraat

(31) Looking for the crème de la crème of vintage furniture? Then step into the living room at **Vintage Home** for furniture from the 1930s to the 1980s. Still in two minds about that purchase? Then book an evening of private dining and kill two birds with one stone: You can enjoy an Italian meal in the store (10 to 35 people), and you have the whole evening to try out 'your' furniture.
daniël stalpertstraat 97, telephone (0031) 020 679 04 72, www.vintagehome.nl, open thurs-sat 11.00-19.00, trams 16, 24, 25 marie heinekenplein

(32) The **Kinderfeestwinkel** is without a doubt the nicest children's store in the neighbourhood. It's just full of dressing up stuff, masks, reading books, picnic things, cuddly toys and loads of other kinds of toys. Brilliant ideas for kids parties.
gerard doustraat 65, telephone (0031) 020 672 22 15, http://kinderfeestwinkel.nl, open mon-fri 10.00-18.00, sat 10.00-17.00, trams 16, 24, 25 marie heinekenplein

(33) **Raak** sells home accessories other gadgets from quality makers. They have beautiful dinner ware, unusual bags and shoes and gorgeous photo albums. Even the tubes of toothpaste and the pedal bins are just that bit different.
eerste van der helststraat 46, telephone (0031) 020 670 42 06, www.raakamsterdam.nl, open ma 12.00-18.00, tues-sat 10.00-18.00, tram 16, 24, 25 marie heinekenplein

(34) It was there long before De Pijp was hip: the **Vredespijp**, 'for buying and selling art-deco and other furniture'. Since then, the shop has expanded and now sells vintage clothes from the 1930s and has a café where the furniture is also for sale.
eerste van der helststraat 11a, telephone (0031) 020 676 48 55, www.vredespijp-artdeco.com, open mon-sat 10.00-18.00, trams 16, 24 albert cuypstraat

34

23

6

5 TASSENMUSEUM HENDRIKJE

Fun things to do

(2) **Pathé Tuschinski** is a lovely cinema to go and catch a film. Reserve a seat on one of the large balconies in the main auditorium so you can enjoy the film, the atmosphere and the architecture of this unique art-deco masterpiece from 1921. Nice idea: VIP and loveseat arrangements.
reguliersbreestraat 26-34, telephone 0900 1458 (€ 0.55 pm), www.pathe.nl/tuschinski, open daily from 11.30, admission € 10, trams 4, 9, 16, 24, 25 muntplein

(5) **Tassenmuseum Hendrikje** (Bag museum Hendrikje) opened its doors in 1996 in a villa in Amstelveen. Nowadays, the collection contains more than four thousand bags and is situated in an imposing building along the Herengracht in Amsterdam. There is the handbag that looks like a telephone, as well as one of those little Swedish purses granny always used to carry. You can even have a go at making your own bag. Call for an appointment.
herengracht 573, telephone (0031) 020 524 64 52, www.tassenmuseum.nl, admission € 6.50, open mon-sunday 10.00-17.00, trams 4, 9, 14 rembrandtplein

(16) Reserve a ticket well in advance and enjoy an evening at **Carré**. Circus director Oscar Carré's former Circus theatre, lovingly renovated in 2004, has, since 1887, blossomed into the most famous theatre in the Netherlands. To honour its one hundred year anniversary, it was given permission to use the title 'Royal'. Check the website for performances, times and prices, or request the programme by phone.
amstel 115-125, telephone (0031) 0900 252 52 55 (daily from 9.00-21.00, € 1.30 per call), www.theatercarre.nl, admission varies, trams 7, 10 weesperplein, metro 51, 53, 54

(20) Wander through the **Albert Cuypmarkt** past all the little stalls and listen to the market folk shouting their wares. Smell the fresh flowers or munch on chips, treacle waffles or herring. It's a great place to buy cheap socks or clothes. Don't forget to look behind the stalls for the nice little shops and places to lunch. The true André Hazes fan obviously has to pay a visit to his statue.
albert cuypstraat, open mon-sat 9.00-17.00, tram 4 stadhouderskade (between the ferdinand bolstraat and the van woustraat), trams 16, 24 albert cuypstraat

Rembrandtplein, Utrechtsestraat & De Pijp

WALK 5

From the Muntplein (1), walk towards the Reguliersbreestraat. Halfway down you'll pass the Pathé Tuschinski (2). You come out onto the Rembrandtplein where you can try the best croquette rolls in the world (3). In Café Schiller (4) you can have a drink amongst real Amsterdammers, a rarity on this square. Turn right into the Utrechtsestraat to do some serious shopping (6) (7) (10) (11) (12) (14). Have a dose of culture on the Heren- en Keizersgracht (5) (8) (9). Turn right into the Utrechtsedwarsstraat, then right again onto the Reguliersgracht. Between the Prinsengracht and the Kerkstraat you'll find Amstelveld. Stop for a drink and a snack (13). Walk behind the little church along the Kerkstraat and cross over the Utrechtsestraat. You'll have a great view of the Magere Brug (15). Cross the bridge, turn right and carry on along the Amstel and admire the Koninklijk Theater Carré (16). Cross over the Sarphatistraat and cross over the water via the Professor Tulpplein and stop for a drink (17). You will pass the elegant Amstel Hotel. Walk on towards the Weesperzijde where you'll find a super terrace (18). Go right, over the bridge: welcome to De Pijp. Cross over the Ceintuurbaan and turn right into the Hemonystraat (19). Turn left into the Hemonylaan. In the distance, you'll see the Albert Cuypmarkt (20). Go inside through the Arabic-Turkish food temple Bazar (21). Fancy cooking these meals at home? Pop along to De Peperbol (22). Just before you reach the end of the market, turn left into the Eerste van der Helststraat for some small bars and shops (23) (24) (25). Turn around and go to the end of the Albert Cuypmarkt. When you get to the end, you'll find a real kitchen paradise to your right on the square (26). Leave the market, and walk along into the Albert Cuypstraat for a gastronomic hamburger (27). Turn right into the beautiful Frans Halsstraat for some really nice little restaurants and shops (28). Turn right at the Jacob van Campenstraat. Still munching on your piece of cake (29) turn into the Ferdinand Bol along the cafés, shops and restaurants (30). Turn left into the Daniël Slapertstraat for vintage furniture (31) or go into the Gerard Doustraat for the Kinderfeestwinkel (32). When you get to the Gerard Douplein, turn left if you want to carry on shopping (33) (34). If not, turn right and have a delicious ice cream (35).

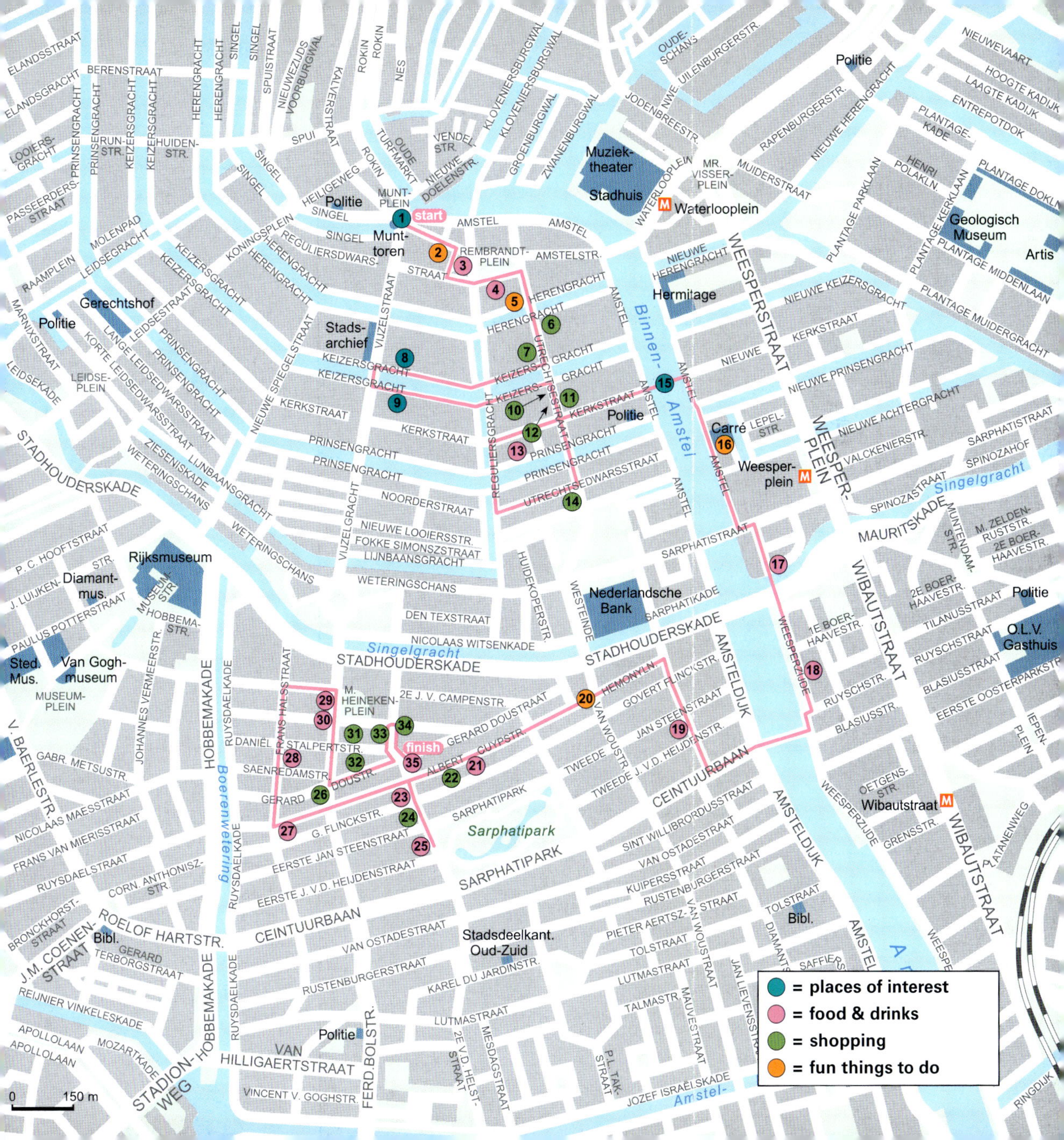

= places of interest
= food & drinks
= shopping
= fun things to do
start
finish
0
150 m
Muntplein
Munttoren
Rembrandtplein
Politie
Stadsarchief
Gerechtshof
Muziektheater
Stadhuis
Waterlooplein
Mr. Visserplein
Hermitage
Geologisch Museum
Artis
Carré
Weesperplein
Rijksmuseum
Diamantmus.
Sted. Mus.
Van Goghmuseum
Museumplein
Nederlandsche Bank
M. Heinekenplein
Sarphatipark
Stadsdeelkant. Oud-Zuid
Bibl.
O.L.V. Gasthuis
Wibautstraat
Binnen-Amstel
Amstel
Singelgracht
Boerenwetering
Elandsstraat
Elandsgracht
Berenstraat
Looiersgracht
Prinsengracht
Runstr.
Keizersgracht
Huidenstr.
Herengracht
Singel
Spuistraat
Nieuwezijds Voorburgwal
Kalverstraat
Rokin
Nes
Spui
Turfmarkt
Oude Turfmarkt
Vendelstr.
Nieuwe Doelenstr.
Kloveniersburgwal
Groenburgwal
Zwanenburgwal
Oudeschans
Nwe Uilenburgerstr.
Jodenbreestr.
Rapenburgerstr.
Muiderstraat
Nieuwe Herengracht
Nieuwevaart
Hoogte Kadijk
Laagte Kadijk
Entrepotdok
Plantage Kade
Henri Polakln.
Plantage Parklaan
Plantage Kerklaan
Plantage Doklaan
Plantage Middenlaan
Plantage Muidergracht
Passeerdersstraat
Heiligeweg
Molenpad
Koningsplein
Reguliersdwarsstraat
Amstelstr.
Raamplein
Leidsegracht
Marnixstraat
Leidsestraat
Leidsekade
Leidseplein
Lange Leidsedwarsstraat
Korte Leidsedwarsstraat
Prinsengracht
Kerkstraat
Vijzelstraat
Vijzelgracht
Nieuwe Spiegelstraat
Utrechtsestraat
Reguliersgracht
Utrechtsedwarsstraat
Stadhouderskade
Weteringschans
Lijnbaansgracht
Ziesenskade
Noorderstraat
Nieuwe Looiersstr.
Fokke Simonszstraat
Den Texstraat
Nicolaas Witsenkade
Huidekoperstr.
Westeinde
Sarphatikade
Sarphatistraat
Amstel
Weesperstraat
Nieuwe Keizersgracht
Nieuwe Prinsengracht
Nieuwe Achtergracht
Lepelstr.
Valckenierstr.
Spinozastraat
Spinozahof
Mauritskade
Muntendamstr.
M. Zeldenrustsstr.
2e Boerhaavestr.
1e Boerhaavestr.
Weesperzijde
Tilanusstraat
Ruyschstraat
Blasiusstraat
Eerste Oosterparkstr.
Iepenplein
Oetgensstr.
Grensstr.
Platanenweg
Ringdijk
Amsteldijk
Hemonyln.
Govert Flinckstr.
Jan Steenstraat
Tweede J. v. d. Heijdenstr.
Tweede
Van Woustr.
Ceintuurbaan
Sint Willibrordusstraat
Van Ostadestraat
Kuiperstraat
Rustenburgerstraat
Pieter Aertszstraat
Tolstraat
Lutmastraat
Talmastr.
Mauvestraat
Jan Lievensstr.
Diamantstr.
Saffierstr.
Jozef Israëlskade
P.L. Takstraat
Mesdagstraat
2e v.d. Helststraat
Lutmastraat
Karel du Jardinstr.
Van Ostadestraat
Ferd. Bolstr.
Van Hilligaertstraat
Vincent v. Goghstr.
Stadion-weg
Hobbemakade
Mozartkade
Apollolaan
Reijnier Vinkeleskade
J.M. Coenenstraat
Bronckhorststraat
Roelof Hartstr.
Gerard Terborgstraat
Ruysdaelkade
Corn. Anthoniszstr.
Ruysdaelstraat
Frans van Mierisstraat
Nicolaas Maesstraat
Gabr. Metsustr.
V. Baerlestr.
Johannes Vermeerstr.
Museumstr.
Hobbemastr.
Paulus Potterstraat
J. Luijkenstr.
P. C. Hooftstraat
Frans Halsstraat
Daniël Stalpertstr.
Saenredamstr.
Gerard Doustr.
G. Flinckstr.
Eerste Jan Steenstraat
Eerste J. v. d. Heijdenstraat
2e J. V. Campenstr.
Gerard Doustraat
Albert Cuypstr.
Sarphatipark

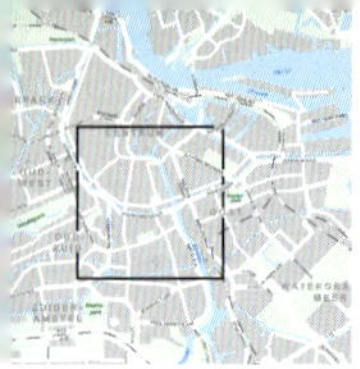

1 De Munt
2 Pathé Tuschinski
3 Van Dobben
4 Café Schiller
5 Tassenmuseum Hendrikje
6 Leonore Sieraden
7 Studio Bazar
8 Foam
9 Museum Van Loon
10 Concerto
11 Look Out
12 Jan
13 Nel
14 A la Carte
15 Magere Brug
16 Carré
17 Amstelhaven
18 Ysbreker
19 Klokspijs
20 Albert Cuypmarkt
21 Bazar
22 De Peperbol
23 Chocolate Bar
24 Tjins
25 Café Krull
26 Duikelman
27 Burgermeester
28 Da Portare Via
29 De Taart van m'n Tante
30 L'Ozio
31 Vintage Home
32 Kinderfeestwinkel
33 Raak
34 Vredespijp
35 IJscuypje

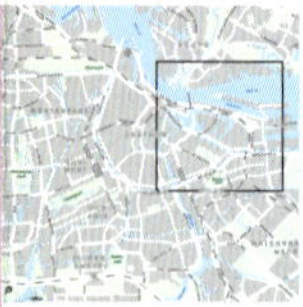

De Eilanden

New, architecture, trail-blazing, different

We all know that clichéd picture of Amsterdam: the old canals, the 17th century stately homes, the brown brickwork, the friendly little bars and that direct Amsterdam sense of humour. But it's not all Old Amsterdam. There's an entirely different side to the city on the Oostelijke Eilanden (Eastern islands) with names like Java, Borneo and KNSM. But the days of the colonies and the Koninklijke Nederlandse Stoomboot Maatschappij KNSM (Royal Dutch Steamboat Company) are long gone: The port of Amsterdam has moved and since the 1990s, these islands have been a centre of creativity and increasingly attractive urban residential areas.

Architects have given their creativity free rein on the Islands and it's a wonderful place to shop for things for your old or modern house, as well as the perfect place for a breath of fresh air on a hot summer's day. This is where the KNSM used to transport cargo and emigrants for so many years. The passenger terminal and old captain's residence on the island still hark back to the old colonial days.

6

galleries. Java is a modern version of the old ring of canals with cosy courtyards and lateral canals. Then there's Borneo. Here, the homes are more inward-orientated towards the indoor gardens.

There is, however, much more to discover. One up and coming neighbourhood is the Czaar Peterbuurt with some great shops, and a walk along the Kalenderpanden is well worth the trouble, not least because you'll get to see some animals in the Artis Zoo for free, like the ibex and zebras. The Plantagebuurt is a haven of peace and affluence. The splendid houses make it perhaps one of the most beautiful neighbourhoods in the city.

It's just a short hop from the Islands to the Amsterdam Hermitage. One of the city's newest attractions isn't actually on the Islands themselves, but it certainly is connected to the history of Amsterdam's shipping trade. This cultural institute, situated in the former Amstelhof Convelescent Home, contains art treasures from faraway places and introduces us to Russia.

6 things not to be missed!

Centrale Bibliotheek

Enjoy the view.

Muziekgebouw aan 't IJ

Experience a concert.

KNSM-eiland

Shopping for your home.

Brouwerij 't IJ

Try one of the upper terraces.

Hermitage

Discover art treasures from Russia

Artis

Stroll around and watch the monkeys.

- **Places of interest**
- **Shopping**
- **Food & drinks**
- **Fun things to Do**

Places of interest

(1) On 7-7-07, the largest library in the Netherlands opened its doors, Amsterdam's **Centrale Bibliotheek**. Visitors from outside the city can't become members, but do have a look inside. The interior design is charming and modern, but it's the view from the restaurant on the seventh floor that makes it worth a visit. A stunning panorama!
oosterdokskade 143, telephone (0031) 020 523 09 00, www.oba.nl, open daily 10.00-22.00, free, trams 1, 2, 4, 5, 9, 13, 16, 17, 24, 25, 26 centraal station

(6) **Pakhuis de Zwijger** has been used as a cold store for perishable goods, a squat and a practice stage for pop musicians (Herman Brood). Now it's one of the last warehouses on this wharf and serves primarily as a platform for culture and media. There is also a café-restaurant with Italian cuisine. So for lunch you could go for freshly filled ciabbatas, and enjoy pizza and pasta in the evening.
piet heinkade 179, telephone (0031) 020 788 44 33, www.dezwijger.nl, open (restaurant) mon-fri 9.00-23.00, trams 25, 26 muziekgebouw bimhuis

(14) By all means, step inside the **Lloyd Hotel**, because this former prison is one of the most unusual places to sleep in Europe. Not many of us get to sleep in a former house of correction every day. The lobby is also a café-restaurant. And they apply the same principle as with the rooms: something to suit every budget.
oostelijke handelskade 34, telephone (0031) 020 561 36 77, www.lloydhotel.com, open (restaurant) 7.00-22.00, trams 10, 26 rietlandpark

(19) Windmills are usually associated with the Kinderdijk rather than Amsterdam, but there are still a couple to be found, like **De Gooyer**, dating from 1725. Unfortunately, you can't go in, but it's still an impressive sight in the middle of the city.
funenkade 5, tram 10 hoogte kadijk

(22) On 1 July 1863, the Netherlands abolished slavery. 139 years later, Queen Beatrix dedicated the **Nationaal Monument Slavernijverleden**. Since then, there has been a memorial service every year, ending with the Keti Koti-festival.
oosterpark (entrance opposite O.L.V. Gasthuis), www.ketikotifestival.nl, trams 3, 7 beukenweg

(23) The **Energetica** museum closed at the end of 2007 ... not enough interest, no support from the local authorities. We are still going to include it though, because it's such a beautiful industrial building, built in 1903. The museum's unique collection, which includes industrial lifts and household appliances, is now housed at NEMO Science Centre, Oosterdok 2. What will happen to the enormous power station itself is still unknown.
hoogte kadijk 400, tram 10 hoogte kadijk

(24) The twelve **Kalenderpanden,** each named after a month of the year, were built in 1840 to form part of the Bonded warehouse. This is where imported goods not destined for Amsterdam were stored temporarily (i.e. in bond). The premises were used as a squat for a while, but now house 44 spacious dwellings. The neo-classical gateway (1830) was also part of the Bonded Warehouse.
entrepotdok 87-98, trams 9, 14 plantage kerklaan

(27) Espionage, safe houses, and illegal newspapers: they are all manifestations of the Dutch Resistance, which are displayed in the **Verzetsmuseum**. By means of ever-changing exhibits the museum also focuses on present day forms of resistance against bigotry and oppression.
plantage kerklaan 61, telephone (0031) 020 620 25 35, www.verzetsmuseum.org, open tues-fri 10.00-17.00, sat-mon & national holidays 11.00-17.00, admission adults € 6.50, children 0-6 years free, 7-15 years € 3.50, trams 9, 14 plantage kerklaan

HERMITAGE AMSTERDAM (34)

NOOIT MEER
AUSCHWITZ
32

19

Hollandsche Schouwburg
Hollandsche Schouwburg
30

(30) The **Hollandsche Schouwburg** was built in 1892 as Amsterdam's fourth theatre. During the Second World War, the Nazis used the concert hall as a deportation centre for Jews. Now it is a monument in memory of all the Dutch Jews who were murdered during the Second World War.
plantage middenlaan 24, telephone (0031) 020 531 03 40, www.hollandscheschouwburg.nl, open daily 11.00-16.00, free , trams 9, 14 plantage kerklaan, metro waterlooplein

(32) The **Wertheimpark** is a small and intimate historic park, a real haven in the city during the day. In 1812, it was the first recreational park in Amsterdam and a gift from Napoleon. Nowadays the park is most famous for the Jan Wolker's Auschwitz monument.
plantage middenlaan, trams 9, 14 plantage kerklaan

(33) The **Hortus Botanicus** dates from 1838 and is therefore one of the oldest in the world. It houses a very exotic mix of six thousand plants from over four thousand species.
plantage middenlaan 2a, telephone (0031) 020 625 90 21, www.hortus-botanicus.nl, open mon-fri 9.00-17.00, sat-sunday & national holidays 10.00-17.00, admission adults € 7, children 5-14 years € 3.50, trams 9, 14 plantage parklaan

(34) The **Hermitage Amsterdam** was opened in grand style by Queen Beatrix and the Russian president Medvedev on 19 June 2009. It is the only branch of St Petersburg's world famous museum outside Russia, with four thousand square metres of art treasures from all over the world. However, the Hermitage is more than just a museum. There are regular workshops and film showings about the rich history of Russia and St Petersburg.
amstel 51, telephone (0031) 020 530 87 51, www.hermitage.nl, admission adults € 15, children to 16 years free, open mon-tues & fri-sunday 10.00-17.00, wed 10.00 to 20.00, trams 9, 14 waterlooplein, metro 51, 53, 54 waterlooplein

Food & drinks

(3) **Star Ferry** is named after the legendary ferry in Hong Kong. Theatre and music lovers aren't the only visitors to the lovely café-restaurant at the Muziekgebouw aan 't IJ, other customers also enjoy the fusion of food-with-a-view.
piet heinkade 1, telephone (0031) 020 788 20 90, www.starferry.nl, open mon-thurs & sunday 10.00-1.00, fri-sat 10.00-2.00, price € 30, trams 25, 26 muziekgebouw bimhuis

(5) The name **Fifteen** immediately conjures up Jamie Oliver. You won't find the TV chef in the kitchen but there will be one of his trainees from a poor background. Enormous, unusual, foody, a bit pricy and unpredictable but still worth having a drink at least. Jamie rules!
in pakhuis amsterdam, jollemanhof 9, telephone (0031) 0900 343 83 36, www.fifteen.nl, open mon-sat 12.00-15.00 & 17.30-22.00, price € 46, tram 26 kattenburgerstraat

(9) Welcome to the old departure hall of the former KNSM, the **Kompaszaal** on the first floor. You can pop in for a drink and every third Sunday in the month there's tango dancing. All that, plus a terrace overlooking the water.
knsm-laan 311, telephone (0031) 020 419 95 96, www.kompaszaal.nl, open wed-sunday 11.00-1.00, tram 10 azartplein

(11) Café-restaurant **Kanis en Meiland** could cautiously be termed the islanders' local. Even so, everyone is welcome to play games, billiards or linger on the terrace and have a beer.
levantkade 127, telephone (0031) 020 418 24 39, www.kanisenmeiland.nl, open sunday-thurs 10.00-1.00, fri-sat 10.00-3.00, tram 10 azartplein, 26 rietlandpark, bus 41, 42 knsm-laan, bus 43 c. van eesterenlaan

KANIS EN MEILAND 11

⑤ **FIFTEEN**

(12) The **Odessa**, named for the Ukrainian city where this ship was built, is one of the jewels of the islands. Above deck you can enjoy an international menu and stunning views; below it's more luxurious and cosy and at the weekend it's party time.
veemkade 259, telephone (0031) 020 419 30 10, www.de-odessa.nl, open wed-thurs 16.00-1.00, fri-sat 16.00-3.00, price € 30, trams 10, 26 rietlandpark

(13) The **Lizboa** is moored next to the trendy Odessa. *La vida* made easy: pay, grab your plate and you're all set. The Spanish and Portuguese dishes are delicious, there's live music and you can eat and dance to your heart's content… quite an experience.
veemkade 251, telephone (0031) 020 419 13 38, www.lizboa.com, open sunday 11.00-22.00, price € 20, trams 10, 26 rietlandpark

(15) Long live **De Cantine**, a real no-nonsense café – and there are not many of those about here – where you can just have a simple meal. At weekends you can just relax and on Sundays there's live music.
rietlandpark 373, telephone (0031) 020 419 44 33, www.decantine.nl, open sunday-thurs 10.00-1.00, fri-sat 10.00-3.00, price € 20, trams 10, 26 rietlandpark

(17) Old fashioned yet trendy. Go to the tiny but super **Helena Primakoff** for breakfast or lunch. Try a sandwich on brown or white bread with some of the unusual fillings: from mackerel with lemon mayonnaise to hummus with sesame seeds and cucumber. Their high teas, chocolate fondue and French toast are fabulous.
czaar peterstraat 135, telephone (0031) 06 48 95 96 94, price € 9, mon-fri 8.30-16.30, sat 10.00-16.30, www.helenaprimakoff.nl, tram 10 eerste leeghwaterstraat

(20) **Brouwerij 't IJ**, next to the De Gooyer windmill, brews the best beer in Amsterdam. Tough luck, Heineken. Beer fanatics come for a 'natte' (double) , 'zatte' (triple) or seasonal beer like 'paasIJ' (spring) or 'IJndejaarsbier' (flavour of the year). Every Friday there's a free tour at 4pm!
funenkade 7, telephone (0031) 020 622 83 25, www.brouwerijhetij.nl, open daily 15.00-20.00, tram 10 hoogte kadijk

(25) You can eat restaurant standard meals at café prices at **Paerz**. You have a choice of meat, fish, vegetarian, charcoal or grill. There's plenty of choice, always simple and organic, and it looks out over the Artis Zoo.
entrepotdok 64, telephone (0031) 020 623 22 06, open tues-sunday 15.00-23.30, price € 25, trams 9, 14 plantage kerklaan

(26) Café-restaurant **Bloem Eten & Drinken** has a waterside terrace, but you can also sit inside in comfort. They serve superior and substantial salads or excellent tournedos with port-wine sauce.
entrepotdok 36, telephone (0031) 020 330 09 29, open daily 12.00-0.00, price € 25, trams 9, 14 plantage kerklaan

(29) Even though **Meneer Nilsson** is called after Pippi Longstocking's monkey, you don't come here for Scandinavian food but for wonderful tapas and more substantial meals from Spain. Relaxed, cheerful and close to the Artis Zoo and the TV studios, which make some well known programmes.
plantage kerklaan 41, telephone (0031) 020 624 48 46, www.meneernilsson.com, open daily 8.30-22.30, price € 25, trams 9, 14 plantage kerklaan

(31) Not trendy or touristy but just **Eik en Linde**. It's a legendary 'bruine kroeg' (old-style pub), from where master interviewer Ischa Meijer used to broadcast his radio programmes. More and more, media people and famous guests from the nearby TV studios frequent the place, as well as biologists from Artis and locals.
plantage middenlaan 22, telephone (0031) 020 622 57 16, www.eikenlinde.nl, open mon-thurs 11.00-1.00, fri-sat 11.00-2.00, prices from € 4, trams 9, 14 plantage kerklaan

29

3

legen in de vrije zone
PAERZ
Timboektoe
kt leverbaar.
Het productschap Paerz adviseert genieten zonder verordeningen, richtlijnen en beschikkingen.
Accijn
25

26

26

7

Shopping

(7) For years now, **Pol's Potten** has been a super interior design shop for the new residents of the islands. They have all the top makes and designers to make your home, garden and kitchen stylish. Do take your credit card though, or you can just go to be inspired.
knsm-laan 39, telephone (0031) 020 419 35 41, www.polspotten.nl, open tues-sat 10.00-18.00, sunday 12.00-17.00, tram 10 azartplein

(8) Skaters of the islands unite. You'll find the latest Vans and Etnies shoes and other street wear at **Arrival/Departure**, a compact but well-stocked lifestyle store. Non-skaters can also enjoy their wonderful mixture of vintage, bohemian-chic clothing and other bits and bobs.
knsm-laan 301, telephone (0031) 020 419 92 34, www.arrivaldeparture.nl, open wed-sat 11.00-18.00, sunday 13.00-18.00, tram 10 azartplein

(16) Go and search for treasure at **De Schatten van Jan en Joop**, a small, original gift shop with something extra: adults can take part in glass workshops and there is an exhibition area for children's art.
czaar peterstraat 143, telephone (0031) 06 27 07 78 48, www.deschattenvanjanenjoop.nl, open tues-sat 10.00-17.30, tram 10 eerste leeghwaterstraat

(18) Thinking about an Arabian-themed party? Finally decided to take belly-dancing classes? Go to the friendly **Jeanines Souk** where you'll find all you need to create A Thousand and One Nights in your own home.
czaar peterstraat 107, telephone (0031) 020 420 55 72, www.buikdanswinkel.nl, open fri 14.00-17.30, sat 12.00-17.30 or call for appointment, tram 10 eerste leeghwaterstraat

Fun things to do

(2) According to its Danish architect, **Muziekgebouw aan 't IJ** is a visiting card made of glass. Since 2005, it has been a superb home for modern and ensemble music.
piet heinkade 1, telephone (0031) 020 788 20 00, www.muziekgebouw.nl, opening times and prices vary, trams 25, 26 muziekgebouw bimhuis

(4) For years, **Bimhuis** was situated in the centre of the city, but in 2005, this Amsterdam platform for jazz and improvised music moved to a spectacular location, which it shares with the Muziekgebouw and Star Ferry. It holds more than 250 jazz-type concerts a year.
piet heinkade 3, telephone (0031) 020 788 21 88, www.bimhuis.nl, opening times and prices vary, trams 25, 26 muziekgebouw bimhuis

(10) The **Souterrain Amsterdam** gallery is one of the few places for experimental modern art. Young artists from various disciplines are given the chance to work together and to gain work experience as curators.
messinastraat 38b, telephone (0031) 020 707 94 85, www.souterrainamsterdam.nl, open thurs-sunday 12.00-17.00, tram 10 azartplein, 26 rietlandpark, buses 41, 42 knsm-laan, bus 43 c. van eesterenlaan

(21) **Studio K** is the hip hang-out in East Amsterdam. A creative, quirky place for film, theatre, food and drink, and music. It all comes together in this former craftsmen's school. Maybe this is a taste of the new East? Its customers are a rich mix of locals, students, artists, young, old, all nationalities. See the website for their programme.
timorplein 62, telephone (0031) 020 692 04 22, www.studio-k.nu, open daily (times vary), tram 3 muiderpoortstation, 7 molukkenstraat, 14 zeeburgerdijk

(28) **Artis** is well worth a visit, even if you don't have kids. As well as providing a home for denizens of the animal world, the zoo is also a haven of peace in the bustling city. Highlights are the aquarium, the planetarium and the ever-entertaining sea lions.
plantage kerklaan 38-40, telephone (0031) 0900 278 47 96, www.artis.nl, open nov-march daily 9.00-17.00, apr-oct daily 9.00-18.00, admission adults € 18.50, children 3-9 years € 15, trams 9, 14 plantage kerklaan

De Eilanden

WALK 6

Exit the Central Station, turn left over the Oosterdokskade via the bus stop. Walk past the new library 1. Turn left towards the waterside. Go right over the bridge, under the railway line till you come to the 't IJ. Cross the little bridge up to the Piet Hein Kade. Walk away from the CS and see the Muziekgebouw aan 't IJ 2, with the café-restaurant Star Ferry 3. Jazz fans will recognise the Bimhuis 4. Carry on walking, then turn left towards the water to the Vrieseveem. Turn right at the end and walk past Jamie Oliver's Fifteen 5. Turn left at the Jan Schaeferbrug. You'll now see the Pakhuis deZwijger 6. Turn right into the Javakade and carry on to the end towards the Azartplein. You are now on Java Island. Glance to your left to see the modern versions of the Amsterdam canals. Shopping time 7 8. Turn right towards the Levantplein then turn right again 9 10. Or have a drink and a snack at Kanis en Meiland 11. Turn left over the Verbindingsdam then turn right onto the Veemkade. You will now see two restaurant ships: the Odessa 12 and the Lizboa 13. Further up on your left is the Lloyd Hotel 14. The De Cantine café just next door is much cosier 15. Via the Rietlandpark, pass under the railway line towards the Czaar Peterstraat, where you'll find a toy shop/children's studio 16, a lunchroom 17 and the 'belly-dance shop' 18. At the end, turn left towards the De Gooyer windmill 19. You can sample the best beer in Amsterdam in the building next door 20. Fancy a shot of art and culture? Carry on to Studio K and the National Monument Slavernijverleden (Slavery Monument) 21 22. Walk back a bit and stroll by Energetica via the Sarphatistraat and Hoogte Kadijk 23. Turn left towards the Entrepotdok and its Calendar buildings 24. Stop off or a drink at Paerz 25 or Bloem 26. At Bloem, turn left over the Nijlpaardenbrug to the Verzetsmuseum 27. The busiest spot is, of course, the Artis Zoo 28. Further along is Meneer Nilsson 29. On the corner, you'll find a dark reminder of Amsterdam's history at the Hollandsche Schouwburg 30 and café Eik en Linde 31.Enjoy the greenery in the Wertheimpark 32 or the Hortus Botanicus 33. Finish off this walk with a visit to the Hermitage 34.

Het IJ
Het IJ
Centraal Station
start
Centraal Station
DE RUYTERKADE
Muziekgebouw aan 't IJ
Bimhuis
IJ-TUNNEL
Centr. Bibl.
Stedelijk Mus. (tijdelijk)
OOSTERDOKSKADE
Oosterdok
NEMO
Scheepvaart-museum
PIET HEINKADE
VEEMKADE
JOLLEMANHOF
VEEMBROEDERHOF
JAVABRUG
JAVAKADE
SUMATRAKADE
TOSARITUIN
TAMAN SARI TUIN
KRATONTUIN
IJhaven
AZARTPLEIN
SURINAMEKADE
KNSM-LAAN
LEVANTKADE
PIREUSPLEIN
VERBINDINGSDAM
Ertshaven
WAAGDRAGERHOF
OOSTELIJKE HANDELSKADE
DIJKSGRACHT
Dijksgracht
MARINIERSKADE
FRED PETTERBAAN
PIET HEINTUNNEL
PANAMALAAN
PANAMAKADE
STUURMANKADE
FEIKE DE BOERLAAN
BORNEOKADE
BORNEOLAAN
C. VAN EESTERENLAAN
Entrepothaven
ENTREPOTKADE
ZEEBURGERKADE
CRUQUIUSWEG
J.M. V.D. MEYLAAN
H.A.J. BAANDERSKADE
ZEEBURGERPAD
Nieuwe Vaart
Lozingskanaal
ZEEBURGERDIJK
Stadsdeelkantoor Zeeburg
KATTENBURGERSTRAAT
KATTENBURGERKADE
GROTE WITTENBURGERSTRAAT
KLEINE WITTENBURGERSTRAAT
WAAIGAT
OOSTENBURGER VOORSTR.
OOSTENBURGERGRACHT
CONRADSTRAAT
CZAAR PETERSTR.
BLANKENSTRAAT
ISAAC TITSINGHKADE
VOC-KADE
Nieuwe Vaart
HOOGTE KADIJK
ENTREPOTDOK
PRINS HENDRIKKADE
NIEUWEVAART
Politie
Waag
Nieuwmarkt
Muziektheater
Stadhuis
Waterlooplein
MUIDERSTR.
PLANTAGE PARKLAAN
PLANTAGE KERKLAAN
PLANTAGE DOKLAAN
PLANTAGE MIDDENLAAN
PLANTAGE MUIDERGRACHT
Geologisch Museum
Artis
Hermitage
finish
Binnen-Amstel
WEESPERSTRAAT
WEESPERPLEIN
Weesperplein
Carré
Politie
NIEUWE KEIZERSGRACHT
NIEUWE PRINSENGRACHT
NIEUWE ACHTERGRACHT
SARPHATISTRAAT
Singelgracht
MAURITSKADE
Tropenmuseum
Oosterpark
OOSTERPARK
LINNAEUSSTRAAT
Stadsdeelkant. Oost, Watergraafsmeer
DAPPERSTRAAT
PONTANUSSTRAAT
CELEBESSTRAAT
SUMATRASTRAAT
JAVASTRAAT
BALISTRAAT
JAVAPLEIN
Politie
MOLUKKENSTR.
Pont-haven
NOORDWAL
Buiksloter Kanaal
Noordhollands Kanaal
0
250 m
= places of interest
= food & drinks
= shopping
= fun things to do

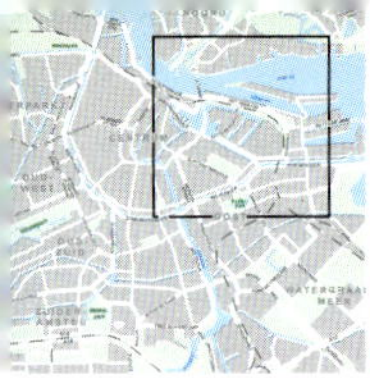

1 Centrale Bibliotheek
2 Muziekgebouw aan 't IJ
3 Star Ferry
4 Bimhuis
5 Fifteen
6 Pakhuis de Zwijger
7 Pol's Potten
8 Arrival/Departure
9 Kompaszaal
10 Souterrain Amsterdam
11 Kanis en Meiland
12 Odessa
13 Lizboa
14 Lloyd Hotel
15 De Cantine
16 De Schatten van Jan en Joop
17 Helena Primakoff
18 Jeanines Souk
19 De Gooyer
20 Brouwerij 't IJ
21 Studio K
22 Nationaal Monument Slavernijverleden
23 Energetica
24 Kalenderpanden
25 Paerz
26 Bloem Eten & Drinken
27 Verzetsmuseum
28 Artis
29 Meneer Nilsson
30 Hollandsche Schouwburg
31 Eik en Linde
32 Wertheimpark
33 Hortus Botanicus
34 Hermitage Amsterdam

Other places of interest

By following the walks in this guide you automatically come across lots of interesting sights. There is, however, so much more to see and to do in Amsterdam, much more than we can possibly describe here. You'll find more information on *www.amsterdam.nl,* the Amsterdam city's website, or *www.nbtc.nl*, the website for the Dutch Bureau for Tourism. Some places of interest and areas that have not been included in the walks, but are still well worth a visit are listed below with short descriptions. You will find the letters next to the names in the general map at the front of this guide.

(M) The **Amsterdam ArenA**, the home ground of Ajax Football Club, is some way away from the centre, but that's no problem for their fans and other football fanatics. The 'World of Ajax' tour will take you around the pitch, the main stands and the press room, among other attractions. If you want to know more, visit the adjoining Ajax Museum where you can learn about the more than 100 year old history of the club. The museum has old photos, cups, trophies and personal belongings of (former) players.
arena boulevard 1 (ajax-stadion), telephone (0031) 020 311 13 33, www.amsterdamarena.nl, see the website for all the opening times and tours, price adults € 9, children 5-8 years € 8, metro 54 strandvliet arena or bijlmer

(N) When you've had enough of the bustle of the city, grab a bike or a bus and go off to the **Amsterdamse Bos**, a nature and recreation park between Amsterdam and Amstelveen. On the edge of the woods, you'll find a number of hockey and football fields There are rowing clubs, and rowing competitions are regularly held on the Bosbaan. It's perfect for walking or cycling. Children head straight for the little goat farm and the pancake house. You can hire a canoe or pedal boat to go on the large pond, and there are two children's paddling pools. One fantastic recurring event is the open-air theatre in July and August, which each summer attracts lots of people. The atmosphere is delightful; people often sit for ages beforehand on the benches with picnic hampers and bottles of wine.
bosbaanweg 5, telephone (0031) 020 545 61 00, www.amsterdamsebos.nl, Visitors Centre open daily 12.00-17.00, free , bus 170, 172 van nijenrodeweg/ amstelveenseweg (from Centraal Station)

This guide has been compiled with the utmost attention to detail. mo'media does not accept responsibility for any inaccuracies. Should you have any comments, please post them on *www.100procentreisgidsen.com* or send them to the address below.

mo'media, o.v.v. 100% amsterdam,
p.o. box 3936, 4800 dx, breda, e-mail info@momedia.nl
www.100procentamsterdam.nl

author revised edition	judith zebeda
author 1st-5th edition	saskia van rijn and tijn kramer
editor	sascha de graaf
translation	sue rixom
editor translation	textcase, utrecht
photography	duncan de fey, www.duncandefey.com sven benjamins, www.svenbenjaminsfotografie.nl marloes bosch, www.marloesboschfotografie.nl saskia van osnabrugge, www.saskiavanosnabrugge.nl
concept design	www.studio100procent.nl, naarden
design	kim peters, www.funkfabriek.nl
lithography	mastercolors mediafactory, eindhoven
project manager	heleen ferdinandusse, mo'media

100% amsterdam isbn 978-90-5767-486-0, nur 510, 511

2nd edition (fully revised) february 2011

(O) As late as the 1960s they were still producing gas on the **Westergasfabriek-terrein** in Amsterdam-West. Now however, it is a nature and (mainly) cultural park on the edge of the city. Many of the historic buildings have been preserved. There is a film theatre showing art house films in the Ketelhuis (boiler house). On the west side, in the former slake processor in the Zuiveringsgebouw, you can eat, drink and dance till the wee small hours in the Pacific Parc. If you want a really special culinary experience, go to the food design studio Proef. See *ww.westergasfabriek.nl* for more information.
ketelhuis, pazzanistraat 4, telephone (0031) 020 684 00 90, www.ketelhuis.nl, opening times vary, tram 10 van limburgstirumplein, pacific parc, polonceaukade 23, telephone (0031) 020 488 77 78, www.pacificparc.nl, open mon-thurs 11.00-1.00, fri-sat 11.00-3.00, sunday 11.00-23.00, tram 10 van limburgstirumplein, proef, gosschalklaan 12, telephone (0031) 020 682 26 56, www.proefamsterdam.nl, open for weddings and other special occasions, tram 10 van limburgstirumplein

(P) Okay, it's hot and you really need to cool down? Then go and visit one of Amsterdam's **city beaches.** They have comfy sofas, real sand and there's always a great party going on. You'll find **Strand Zuid** in Amsterdam Zuid on the edge of the Beatrixpark. Here it's all about glitter, glamour and lots of scooters. For a more relaxed atmosphere, try the **Strand West**, in Amsterdam West. Do you fancy a swim as well as just chilling? Then take a dip in the IJ at **Blijburg aan Zee**. The lifeguard keeps an eye on the children, while Mum and Dad enjoy a mojito. This area is being developed so rapidly that it's uncertain how long the beach at IJburg will remain. And don't miss **BovenNEMO**, a large terrace on the roof of the NEMO science center. No beach sand, but a fantastic watery playground for the kids and spectacular views over the city.
strand zuid: europaplein 22, telephone (0031) 020 544 59 70, www.strand-zuid.nl, open daily 10.00-0.00, tram 4, metro 50, sneltram 51 rai, strand west: stavangerweg 900, telephone (0031) 020 682 63 10, www.strand-west.nl, open mon-sunday 10.00-23.00, bus 22, 48 spaardammerstraat,blijburg aan zee: bert haanstrakade 2004, telephone (0031) 020 416 03 30, www.blijburg.nl, opening times vary, tram 26 eindhalte IJburg, bovennemo: oosterdok 2, telephone (0031) 020 531 31 50, opening times vary, www.e-nemo.nl, free , open 27 june-6 sep daily 12.00-19.30, trams 1, 2, 4, 5, 9, 13, 16, 17, 24, 25 , 26 centraal station

Going out

When it comes to having a night out, Amsterdam offers so many choices. Film, theatre, plays, music, dance and comedy: it's all there. For a really comprehensive guide to what's on, you could look at PS, Het Parool's Saturday supplement or the free fortnightly magazine NL20. The Amsterdams Uitburo, on the corner of the Leidseplein/Marnixstraat, is also a good place to start (open mon-wed & fri-sat 10.00-18.00, thurs 10.00-21.00). They supply cultural information as well as selling tickets for concerts, sometimes (last minute) even at half-price. You'll find a list of the major festivals on pages 5 and 6. Below you'll find a selection from the countless bars and clubs in Amsterdam; the letters correspond to those on the general map at the front of this guide. To avoid any disappointment it's well worth the effort to check what's on each evening before you go out. Keep an eye open for all the flyers from the clubs that you'll find in various shops and record stores.

(Q) Bar/club **Bitterzoet** has blossomed into one of *the* trend-setting entertainment places in Amsterdam. The outstanding DJs, fantastic atmosphere, a really varied mix of music styles – from punk to hip-hop and rock to soul, make this not-too-big bar/club a really great place to party. Do bear in mind though, it's always heaving.
spuistraat 2, telephone (0031) 020 421 23 18, www.bitterzoet.com, open mon-thurs & sunday 20.00-3.00, fri-sat 20.00-4.00, admission varies, trams 1, 2, 5, 13, 17 nieuwezijds kolk

(R) **Jazzcafé Alto** is one of the best jazz cafés in Amsterdam. In this intimate and cosy bar, Hans Dulfer is on stage every Wednesday evening. During the rest of the week, you can enjoy other well- and less well-known musicians.
korte leidsedwarsstraat 115, telephone (0031) 020 626 32 49, www.jazz-cafe-alto.nl, open mon-thurs & sunday 21.00-3.00, fri-sat 21.00-4.00, free, trams 1, 2, 5, 7, 10 leidseplein

Ⓢ **Paradiso** can be found in a neo-Gothic church and offers something different every night of the week: jazz, fusion, latin, funk, garage, ska and deep soul. One classic is Noodlanding! on Wednesday evenings when they have live performances, cabaret and new disco. From time to time, Paradiso also plays host to some big names. The Rolling Stones, David Bowie, Prince and Lenny Kravitz are just some of the stars who have performed here. *weteringschans 6-8, telephone (0031) 020 626 45 21, www.paradiso.nl, open wed-thurs 23.00-3.00, fri-sat 0.00-4.00, admission varies, trams 1, 2, 5, 7, 10 leidseplein*

Ⓢ **PARADISO**

Ⓣ For the less mainstream happenings, try the **Melkweg**. There are two main halls (Max and Oude Zaal), and it's a place that really rocks at the weekends. Regularly, there are special events, such as the Jazz & Fusion concert, the SupaSonic Festival and the Amsterdam Dance Event. The Melkweg also houses a gallery, a small cinema, a theatre and a media room for new media.
lijnbaansgracht 234a, telephone (0031) 020 531 81 81, www.melkweg.nl, opening times vary (café open daily from 10.00, venue usually open from 21.00), admission varies, trams 1, 2, 5, 7, 10 leidseplein

(u) You'll find **Arena Tonight** near the Oosterpark, inside a former church. The music in this rather imposing yet intimate dance hall varies from house, club and R&B to top 40 hits. If you want to roll into bed straight from dancing till the small hours, make sure to book a room beforehand in the adjoining Hotel Arena.
's gravesandestraat 51, telephone (0031) 020 850 24 00, www.hotelarena.nl, open fri & sat 23.00-4.00, admission varies, tram 10 korte 's gravesandestraat, 9, 14 Mauritskade, 3 Beukenweg

(v) Do you want to go dancing in the trendiest club in Amsterdam? Then you really must try **Jimmy Woo**. There's always a long queue at the door. Inside, the dominant colour is black. The walls are covered in gold foil, there are Chinese antiques everywhere and at least 12, 000 lights sparkle down from the ceiling. Add the excellent national and international DJs plus a cocktail bar to the mix, and you are sure to have a fantastic night.
korte leidsedwarsstraat 18, telephone (0031) 020 626 31 50, www.jimmywoo.com, open thurs & sunday 23.00-3.00, fri-sat 23.00-4.00, admission varies, trams 1, 2, 5, 6, 7, 10 leidseplein

(w) In the 'chic' **Zebra Lounge** with its red couches and gigantic chandelier in the centre of the club, a variety of DJs provide some very laid-back entertainment. Two floors, with latin, urban, house, and disco give you plenty to choose from in these seductive surroundings.
korte leidsedwarsstraat 14, telephone (0031) 020 612 61 53, www.the-zebra.nl, open daily 22.00-4.00, admission varies, trams 1, 2, 5, 7, 10 leidseplein

(x) In a former factory on the Oostelijke Handelskade you'll find **Panama**. You can have a complete evening out here: first, a nice drink and a meal in the restaurant and then either a theatre performance and/or dancing till the wee hours. They have brilliant DJs and sometimes there is live music.
oostelijke handelskade 4, telephone (0031) 020 311 86 86, www.panama.nl, open thurs 23.00-3.00, fri-sat 23.00-4.00, admission varies, sunday 23.00-1.00, tram 10 rietlandpark

Alphabetical index

index by theme

hotels

fun things to do

shopping

going out

transport